THE RHÔNE VALLEY & SAVOY

PASSPORT'S REGIONAL GUIDES OF FRANCE

Series Editor: Arthur Eperon

Auvergne and the Massif Central
Rex Grizell

Brittany
Frank Victor Dawes

The Dordogne and Lot
Arthur and Barbara Eperon

Languedoc and Roussillon
Andrew Sanger

The Loire Valley
Arthur and Barbara Eperon

Normandy, Picardy and Pas de Calais
Barbara Eperon

Paris
Vivienne Menkes-Ivry

Provence and the Côte d'Azur
Roger Macdonald

South West France
Andrew Sanger

THE RHÔNE VALLEY & SAVOY

Rex Grizell

Photographs by David Ward

PASSPORT BOOKS
a division of *NTC Publishing Group*

Title page illustration: Stone carving at
Les Baux-de-Provence.

This edition first published in 1991 by Passport Books,
a division of NTC Publishing Group, 4255
West Touhy Avenue, Lincolnwood (Chicago), Illinois
60646-1975 U.S.A. Originally published by
Christopher Helm (Publishers) Ltd.,
a subsidiary of A & C Black (Publishers) Ltd.,
35 Bedford Row, London, England.
Copyright © Rex Grizell 1991.
Photographs by David Ward.
Line illustrations by David Saunders.

Printed and bound in Singapore.

Contents

1 Introduction   1

    The Weather — When and Where To Go   4

    General information and useful addresses   6

    Conversion Tables   7

2 Some History   8

    History of the River   12

3 Food and Wine   19

4 Savoy   23

5 Lyon and the Lyonnais   45

6 Ardèche   75

7 Isère   99

8 Drôme   121

9 Around Avignon   141

Index   176

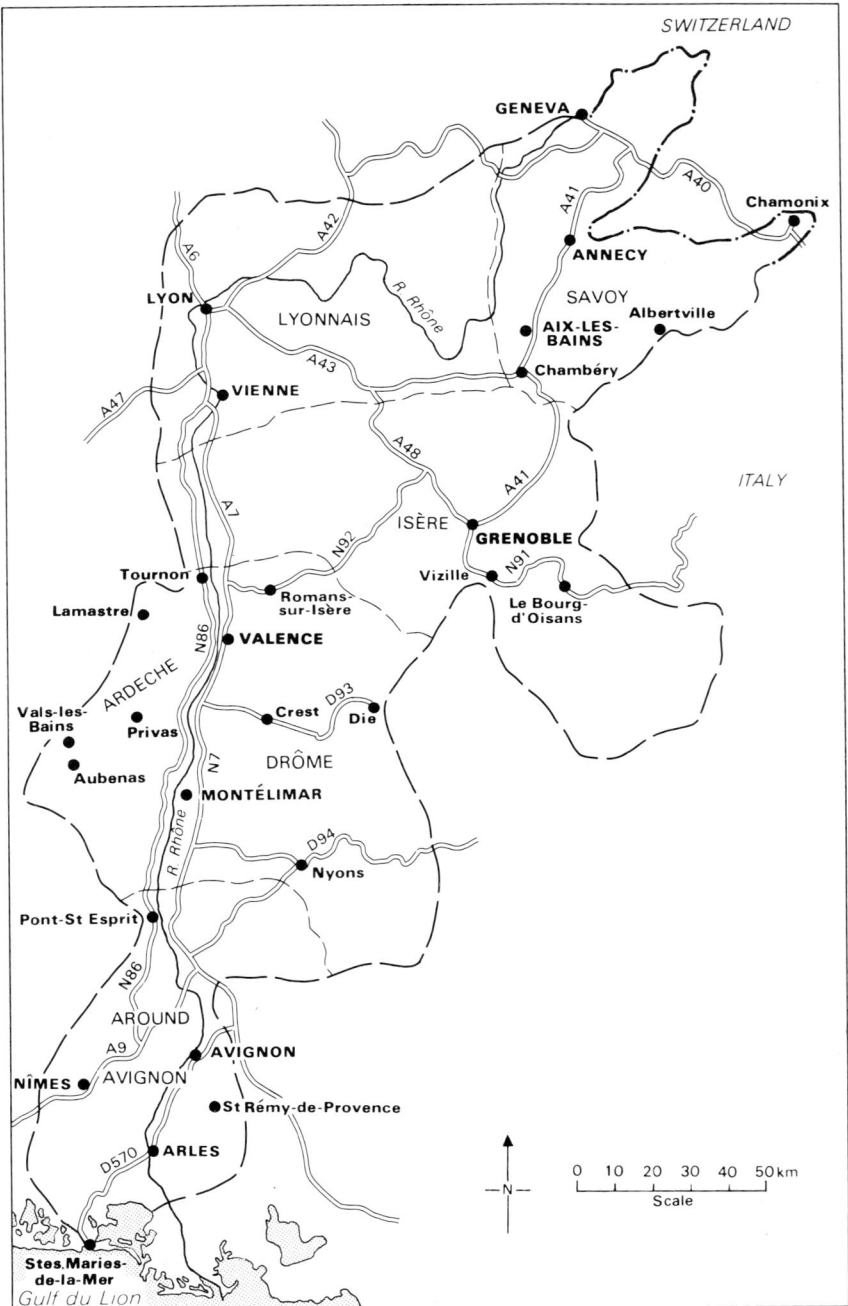

SWITZERLAND

GENEVA

A40

A41

Chamonix

A42

ANNECY

SAVOY

AIX-LES-BAINS

Albertville

A6

LYON

LYONNAIS

R. Rhône

Chambéry

A43

VIENNE

A47

A48

ISÈRE

GRENOBLE

A41

A7

N92

N91

ITALY

Tournon

Romans-sur-Isère

Vizille

Le Bourg-d'Oisans

Lamastre

N86

VALENCE

Vals-les-Bains

Privas

Crest

D93

Die

ARDECHE

DRÔME

Aubenas

N7

MONTÉLIMAR

R. Rhône

D94

Nyons

Pont-St Esprit

N86

AROUND

AVIGNON

A9

AVIGNON

NÎMES

St Rémy-de-Provence

D570

ARLES

N

0 10 20 30 40 50km
Scale

Stes.Maries-de-la-Mer

Gulf du Lion

1
Introduction

Among all its natural beauties – the verdant forests, the countless lakes, the rugged coasts, the vine-covered slopes, the mountains, from the High Alps to the old volcanoes of the Massif Central and on to the lovely Pyrenees – nothing contributes more to the image of La Belle France than its rivers. It is hardly possible to think of France without calling to mind a river. The lazy, courtly Loire, reflecting a fleet of small, white summer clouds; the clear sprightly, sunlit Dordogne; the Tarn and its dark, spectacular gorges; and all those peaceful, poplar-lined rivers where anglers live their private, impenetrable dreams; all these together create the variety and the harmony of the French landscape.

Of all these hundreds of rivers there is one which is unlike any other, the Rhône. Known for centuries as *le Rhône sauvage* – the wild Rhône – it is more a huge mountain torrent than an average river, but after many years and at great expense its ferocity has now been largely tamed by the ingenuity and persistence of French engineers. The towns on its banks are no longer disastrously flooded, nor its bridges and villages carried away by the tearing anger of its current. It is today a river of considerable variety and often of dramatic beauty, some-

times flowing through rocky defiles, sometimes through wide valleys rich with vineyards and peach orchards, sometimes overlooked by ruined castles, witnesses of a long and turbulent past, sometimes by great cathedrals in cities where the history of religion was forged.

The Rhône rises in Switzerland in the Massif of St Gothard, not the highest but the most extensive of all the glacial massifs of the Alps. It flows for 140km through the canton of Valais, and into Lake Geneva (Lac Leman). From the high mountains on both sides countless torrents descend to increase the force and volume of the river. It is said that 260 glaciers contribute to its growth. All the way to the lake it has the impetuous character of a mountain torrent, foaming down steep slopes, over waterfalls, through boulder-strewn ravines, and with a fall of nearly 1,400m.

The river, which brings down 330,000m^3 of rock, stones and soil into Lake Geneva every year will eventually fill it completely, although this will take about 200,000 years. On average it carries 15 times as much water into the lake in summer, as the snows melt, as it does in winter.

The Rhône, clean and purified, having left all its rubble in the lake,

1

flows out into France through a narrow ravine, the only possible route between the mountains of the Jura to the north and the Savoy Alps to the south. Until 1860, when Savoy became part of France, this defile was of great strategic importance and was protected by two forts on the Jura side. The place is still called Fort d'Ecluse. The gorge is so narrow and precipitous that if it were suddenly blocked, the back-up of the waters of the Rhône would submerge the whole of the city of Geneva including its hills. The danger was shown in January 1883 when, after prolonged rains, there was a landslide which completely blocked the river's path. Part of the Lyon–Geneva railway line and a tunnel were carried away. Downstream of the fall the bed of the river became dry, and behind the mass of earth and rocks the river rose, overflowing its banks, drowning houses and forming a lake several kilometres long. But the tremendous force of the pent-up water gradually broke through the debris, and the Rhône resumed its course, although the main railway line was blocked for months.

This was just one incident in a career of violence. In historic times the Rhône flooded so frequently that only the most terrible years were recorded. As the centuries passed the story was always the same – ferries sunk, ships wrecked, people drowned, then bridges carried away, villages destroyed, banks and towpaths broken down, towns under water. It was all still happening in the early part of this century. In 1910 Lyon, Tournon and Valence, were so heavily flooded that people had to take to boats. It was the same story in 1928.

Not surprisingly, with all this force behind it, the river takes an erratic course, frequently changing direction and often dividing into two or three channels. From Fort d'Ecluse where it enters France, the river flows at first through sheer-sided ravines, often as much as 200m deep. At Bellegarde it turns sharply south. There was a place near here called La Perte du Rhône where the river poured into a chasm only a few feet across and disappeared in huge clouds of spray into a hole at the bottom, only to burst out again little more than 100m further on. This spot was a popular destination for outings and people liked to be photographed standing on rocks beside the clouds of spray, but when the barrage at Génissiat, a few miles further south, was constructed in the late thirties, La Perte du Rhône was lost beneath the lake formed behind the barrage.

All the way to Anthon, where it is joined by a major tributary, the Ain, 30km from Lyon, the Rhône rings the changes on wide valleys, narrow gorges, marshy flats, and as many as four different channels separated by islands large and small.

In the centre of Lyon the moody and violent Rhône receives the important but much calmer tributary, the Saône, and from Lyon south to the Mediterranean, 340km, it is a wide, impressive river, powerful still, but disciplined by man. Unlike the upper reaches, where the river flows through unspoiled countryside with hardly a town of any size on its banks, this stretch of the Rhône has its fair share of power stations, industry and engineering works. But, paradoxically, it is this middle Rhône that tourists come to see, because it also has far more than its fair share of beauty and historic interest, a series of wonderful old towns strung along its banks like jewels on a silver cord. Lyon, Vienne, Valence, Tournon, Orange, Avignon, Arles – what a parade of ancient splendour they offer: Roman temples and arenas, Norman and Gothic churches, ruined castles, cloistered abbeys and streets of medieval and Renaissance houses.

Despite all that has been done to tame it, this middle section of the Rhône retains a powerful and impetuous character, partly due to the steepness of its fall. It repeatedly divides into different channels, either naturally or where canals have been made to make navigation easier, and it is scattered with islands, some permanent and others which come and go according to the whims of the temperamental currents.

Between Tournon and Valence it is joined by the Isère, an important river which rises in the glaciers of the Alps near the Italian border and flows through Grenoble on its way to join the Rhône.

At Pont-St Esprit, the Ardèche, a river which in times of flood has been known to rise 20m in one day, comes in from the north-west. As the Rhône approaches Avignon, it twists and turns, creating more large islands. South of the former papal city it is joined by the Durance, a river of such ferocity that in flood it delivers 170 times as much water to the Rhône as it does when it is low. After this confluence the river becomes much wider and at Arles, for the last part of its journey to the sea through the department of Bouches du Rhône, it divides into two, the Grand and the Petit Rhône. The two branches enter the Mediterranean some 25km apart, the Petit Rhône near Stes Marie-de-la-Mer and the Grand Rhône to the east

between Port-St Louis-du-Rhône and Port-de-Fos. Between these two branches lies the last of the Rhône's many surprises, the mysterious land of the Camargue. The home of white horses, black bulls and pink flamingos, a maze of lakes and intersecting waterways, of mud flats and marshes, the Camargue has some patches of shoddy tourism but the Parc Naturel Regional de Camargue remains a paradise for accredited naturalists.

For almost all of its 600km in France the Rhône Valley has wild upland or beautiful mountain scenery on both sides. These lovely and little-known regions are included in this guide, in addition to the river valley and its historic towns. In the north there are the high mountains and scenic lakes of the former kingdom of Savoy. Around Lyon there are the vineyards and rolling hills of Beaujolais, and the picturesque old villages of the Lyonnais. To the west, as the river flows due south, are the plateaux and hills of Ardèche, flanking the Massif Central, and the wonderful scenery of the Gorges de l'Ardèche. On the east, in the departments of Isère and Drôme, there is some of the wildest and least-visited countryside in France, rising from the valley orchards and vineyards to the remote plateau of Vercors, and on to range after range of majestic mountains. Further south the river flows between the departments of Gard and Vaucluse and through the luminous, sunscorched landscape of Provence, studded with souvenirs of the rich Roman past, the Middle Ages and the Renaissance and leaves behind it a roll-call of historic names: Avignon, Arles, Les Baux de Provence, Nîmes, Orange, the Pont du Gard.

Down the length of the river the way of life, the traditions and beliefs and even the language of the people differ from region to region. The climate changes, different crops are produced, the wines and the style of cooking are regional and widely varied. The architectural styles of houses and churches, and the materials used in their construction, vary from one place to the next and from one bank of the river to the other. In all this variety and changing scenery the presence of the great river is the only unifying factor.

From its source in the frozen heights of the Alps to the Mediterranean shore is a long way, but the appeal of the Rhône Valley is that no matter what section the visitor chooses it will have its own unforgettable sights, its own colourful history, its own scenic beauty, and, though there will be many facilities for holiday visitors, it will still be a genuine place with its own individual style.

The Weather and When To Go

Although the regions described in this book are all in southern France, the weather varies according to how far south they are, how close to the Mediterranean, and also on their altitude and distance from the Rhône itself.

Savoy and Isère are both in the northern part of the area and very mountainous. The climate here is alpine, unaffected by the Mediterranean. The winters are cold and snow remains all year round on slopes above 2,500 metres. There are some winter sports resorts, Les Tignes for example, where it is normally possible to ski throughout the year. The best months for a non-skiing holiday in the mountains are from June to mid-September, when sunshine and warm days are predominant. As in almost all mountain areas some showers and thunderstorms can be expected, particularly in July and August, and often after midday.

Temperatures in the Lyon area are warm throughout the summer, but rarely extreme. In spring and autumn the presence of the two big rivers leads to fairly frequent thick mists in the city.

As you go south from Lyon the climate becomes steadily warmer and sunnier, and from Valence southwards it is typically Mediterranean. The summers in Ardèche, Drôme, and Provence are frankly and reliably hot. During the rest of the year the climate of the south is unpredictable. There can be warm spells at any time, but also cold periods, though rarely very cold. Long periods of rain are uncommon but, typically, there are some heavy rainstorms in spring and autumn, both inland and on the coast.

The notorious wind of the Rhône Valley, the mistral, blows for the most part between October and April. Summer visitors are not likely to be bothered by it, but in winter the mistral — its name comes from the Latin *magister* and means master wind — can blow with tremendous force. It screams down the Rhône Valley from the north-west, with gusts reaching 200k.p.h., tearing out trees, stripping roofs, blowing away cars. It is icily cold and goes on for days, putting everyone's nerves on edge. But the mistral has its merits. It blows away clouds and dust, and keeps the skies of Provence crystal clear. In the past it was credited with preventing the fevers and diseases of the swamps of the Rhône delta from spreading up the valley, by blowing the miasmic vapours out to sea. Today it clears away traffic fumes and the smoke of power stations and factories, and heralds sunny weather.

General Information and Useful Addresses

TOURIST OFFICES The address of the main Tourist Office or Syndicat d'Initiative for each department is given at the end of the relevant chapter. But there is a tourist office or syndicat in every town, and in the villages the Mairie will be happy to answer queries from tourists. In most towns these days there is someone in the Tourist Office who speaks reasonable English. These offices exist to help tourists and visitors should not hesitate to make use of them.

HOTELS Where possible the hotels listed at the end of each chapter include a large one where overnight travellers who have not booked ahead have the best chance of finding a room. But in the summer high season tourists are strongly advised to reserve at least a day in advance.

RESTAURANTS Recommended restaurants are also listed at the end of each chapter. In small towns and villages in southern France the midday meal is the most important one of the day and starts promptly at twelve noon. The later you arrive the less likely you are to find space, and the more likely to find a reduced menu. Reserve ahead if you can.

BANKS Approximate hours 09.00–16.00. Closed two hours for lunch and on either Saturdays or Mondays (if one is closed, the nearest of the same group will be open). Branches in small towns and villages may not change travellers' cheques.

For specialist leisure attractions, see the addresses given in the listed information after each chapter; the following may also be useful:

WALKING HOLIDAYS Comité National des Sentiers de Grandes Randonnées, 92 rue de Clignancourt, 75883 Paris.

RIDING AND PONY TREKKING L'Association Nationale pour le Tourisme Equestre, 15 rue de Bruxelles, 75009 Paris.

FISHING Conseil Supérieur de la Pèche, 10 rue Peclet, 75015 Paris.

CYCLING Fédération Française de Cyclotourisme, 8 rue Jean Marie Jego, 75013 Paris.

A letter to one of these organisations will bring details of local addresses in the areas which interest you.

COUNTRY COTTAGES Fédération Française des Gîtes Ruraux, 35 rue Godot de Mauroy, 75009 Paris. Or from the French Government Tourist Office, 178 Picaddilly, London W1V OAL.
Several British tour operators offer package holidays in country cottages (gîtes), e.g. VFB Holidays, Normandy House, High Street, Cheltenham, GL50 3HW.

Conversion Tables

km	miles	km	miles	km	miles
1	0.62	8	4.97	40	24.86
2	1.24	9	5.59	50	31.07
3	1.86	10	6.21	60	37.28
4	2.48	15	9.32	70	43.50
5	3.11	20	12.43	80	49.71
6	3.73	25	15.53	90	55.93
7	4.35	30	18.64	100	62.14

m	ft	m	ft	m	ft
100	328	600	1,968	1,500	4,921
200	656	700	2,296	2,000	6,562
300	984	800	2,625	2,500	8,202
400	1,313	900	2,953	3,000	9,842
500	1,640	1,000	3,281	3,500	11,483

ha	acres	ha	acres	ha	acres
1	2.5	10	25	100	247
2	5	25	62	150	370
5	12	50	124	200	494

kg	lbs	kg	lbs
1	2.2	6	13.2
2	4.4	7	15.4
3	6.6	8	17.6
4	8.8	9	19.8
5	11.0	10	22.0

°C	°F	°C	°F	°C	°F
0	32	12	54	24	75
2	36	14	57	26	79
4	39	16	61	28	82
6	43	18	64	0	86
8	46	20	68	32	90
10	50	22	72	34	93

2
Some History

The valley of the Rhône was, in the distant past, the most important economic and political route in the development of Western Europe. Civilisation spread westwards along the coasts of the Mediterranean, and its first penetration towards the north was made via the Rhône Valley long ago. The Phoenicians, the Greeks and the Romans all took this route into the heart of France, and in turn brought with them their culture, their arts and their religious beliefs. After them came a long succession of conquerors and traders. It was on the banks of· the Rhône that the first elegant cities of the west were built, and it was in its valley that some of the most significant events of French history took place.

Even before Roman times, Phoenician and Greek merchants preferred the difficulties of the Rhône route to the greater risks of the long voyage through the Straits of Gibraltar, all round the Iberian Peninsula and across the stormy Bay of Biscay to Cornwall. Instead they sailed as far as they could up the Rhône, to the point where Lyon stands today. There they transferred to wagons to cross central Gaul, either to the Seine, the Loire or the Rhine, then back into boats as far as the estuaries of these rivers, where they met British traders and exchanged their goods from the Middle East and the Mediterranean shores for Cornish tin.

The Phoenicians established small trading posts at several points on the Rhône, but the first real settlement was made by Greeks from the region of Corinth. They built a town on the coast near the mouth of the river and called it Massalia. Later the Romans captured it and called it Massilia. Today it is Marseilles.

In their conquest and administration of Gaul the Romans used the same routes as these earlier traders. Caesar's legions occupied most of the valley in 58BC. The Celts who already inhabited the region were a savage and bloodthirsty race, uncultured and given to sacrifice, drunkenness, and tribal warfare. Some of their habits were less than charming, like cutting off the heads of their enemies and nailing them to their doors to show off to visitors. They were ruled by a brutal and quarrelsome military aristocracy who spent their time in orgies and feasts when not fighting. But belligerent as they were, their resistance against the greater military skills and discipline of the Romans was ineffective.

The victorious Romans used the Celtic capital, Vienne, as an administrative centre, but though the Celts had been beaten in the Rhône Valley as a whole, those in the area around Vienne refused to sit quietly. They rose up and attacked the Roman settlers, putting them to flight. It was this dispute which led to the official founding of Lyon in 43BC. The Senate in Rome ordered a general called Plancus to resettle the refugees from Vienne at a place at the confluence of the Rhône and the Saône, where there had been a small trading post since about 500BC. They called the new town Lugdunum, now Lyon.

After the assassination of Julius Caesar, the struggle for power was won by his adopted son, Octavius, who, calling himself Augustus, became Emperor in 27BC. He gave the job of organising Gaul to his friend and son-in-law Agrippa, who ensured the future prosperity of the region by building five great roads linking the Rhône Valley to the rest of Europe.

For more than 300 years the area enjoyed all the benefits of Roman planning and controlled government. They made Lyon the local capital, and here and in the other towns of the region, they built the theatres, temples, spas, villas, arches, arenas and other monuments so characteristic of their civilisation, the remains of which are still imposing after 2,000 years.

In the 4th century the Roman Empire in the west began to crumble as a result of weak central government combined with repeated attacks by Germanic tribes from the north-east. The emperors lost interest in the province and in the 5th century the Burgondes, who were to give their name to Burgundy, occupied the Rhône Valley and settled in Lyon and Vienne. But their power came to an end in

Statue of Augustus in the Proscenium wall at the Roman theatre, Orange

500AD, when they were defeated by another Germanic race, the Franks, under the leadership of Clovis. He was the chief who founded the first royal house of France, the Merovingians.

During the Dark Ages and early medieval times the whole of what is now south-eastern France was continually fought over by lawless barons who gained and lost huge estates according to the fortunes of war.

The only constant factor in these long centuries was the steady rise of the Church, as more abbeys were founded and more churches and cathedrals built. It was not until the 11th century that the power of the

9

Kingdom of France began to be felt in the region, but it amounted to no more than occasional influence, not government.

Gradually the area became more prosperous, and during the 13th and 14th centuries royal power in the valley of the Rhône was consolidated. An important development was the establishment, by royal decree in 1419, of the international fairs in Lyon. These attracted merchants from all over Europe and the Mediterranean, considerably increased trade and activity in the Rhône Valley, and gave Lyon a commercial importance which, despite fluctuations, it has never lost.

The religious wars between Catholics and Protestants strongly affected the Rhône Valley, where Protestantism had been well received, throughout the 16th century. A number of important towns, including Lyon, were captured by the Protestants in the 1550s and 1560s and later recaptured by the Catholics.

When King Henri II of France was accidentally killed in a friendly joust in 1559, his widow, Catherine de Medici, who had three under-age sons, ruled as regent throughout the early part of the religious wars. She was tolerant and at first tried to settle the conflict without bloodshed. It was part of her tactics to use a 'flying squad' of beautiful and aristocratic girls whose job it was to 'persuade' influential Protestant leaders to change their beliefs. The savagery of the struggle was largely due to the fact that many noble and powerful families, whose members included generals and admirals, had been converted to

The temple of Augustus, Roman emperor in the first century BC, at Vienne

the new faith. Catherine was following the same 'persuasive' policy in arranging the marriage of her daughter, Marguerite de Valois, to Henri III, King of Navarre, a Protestant. The marriage took place at Notre Dame cathedral in Paris on 18 August 1572. Six days later, Charles IX, who had come of age and had been ruling for a year, authorised the St Bartholomew's Day massacre in which 4,000 Protestants were killed.

Charles IX died of tuberculosis in 1574, and was succeeded by Catherine's third son, who became Henri III of France (not to be confused with his brother-in-law, Henri III of Navarre). The new King of France liked wearing dresses, used make-up to improve his complexion. and wore gloves in bed to preserve the delicacy of his hands. His depravities left him little time for matters of state, and he had no religious faith himself, but he felt things should continue as they were, so he gave the Catholic leaders a free hand against the Protestants, and the bitter fighting continued.

Though he had no interest in women, Henri III had married in the hope of producing an heir. but he remained childless. When he was assassinated in 1610, the Valois dynasty, which had ruled France for nearly 300 years, came to an end. The heir to the throne was Henri III of Navarre, the son-in-law of Catherine de Medici, who was a direct descendant of Louis IX of France. But he was a Protestant, and the Catholics would have preferred a republic to a Protestant monarchy. Henri, however, put an end to their opposition by turning Catholic. He became Henri IV of France, and was in the end the most popular of all French kings.

The religious wars were brought to an end when Henri signed the Edict of Nantes in 1589, allowing the Protestants considerable freedom of worship. But in 1610 he was assassinated. He had divorced Marguerite de Valois, and married Marie de Medici, another daughter of Catherine. Her rule as regent during the minority of her son, Louis XIII was indecisive, but when he came of age, he himself led Catholic troops against the Protestants, and the religious wars broke out again. In the Rhône Valley the new disturbances were of minor importance.

During the latter half of the 17th century the religious enmity gradually simmered down and the 100 years leading up to the French Revolution was a period of commercial expansion for the towns of the Rhône. But all that changed in 1793 when the citizens of Lyon, who at first had been in favour of the Revolution, turned against it and executed one of its officials. In retaliation the troops of the revolutionary government, the Convention, attacked the city. Much of the centre was destroyed, and thousands of its citizens were put to death.

In Napoleonic times the towns of the Rhône Valley began a long period of expansion which has continued until the present day.

During the Second World War the French Resistance movement was strong in the region around Lyon. In the remote fastnesses of the plateau of Vercors, the troops of the Maquis were trained in sabotage, and attacks against the German occupying forces were planned. Several thousand men were ready to take action against the Germans, but they were forestalled. The Germans learned of the extent of the opposition building up and struck first with paratroops. Three villages were destroyed and 700 of the inhabitants of Vercors lost their lives.

During the past 40 years the history of the Rhône Valley area has been one of a steady increase in prosperity, in which tourism has played a significant part.

History of the river

The river Rhône has its own colourful history, distinct from the history of the region. It has always been navigable for about half its length, from just north of Lyon to the sea, though with considerable risk and difficulty. Its fast-flowing current, its tendency to flood, sometimes disastrously, in spring and early summer, its shallowness in places in other seasons, and its constantly changing channels combined to make it a dangerous river. But men were obliged to tackle it from earliest times because its course was the only route between the tangled heights of the Massif Central and the even more mountainous country to the east. Not only that, the Rhône led directly to other major routes, north-west to Paris, north-east by the Belfort Gap to the Rhine and Germany, and east to Switzerland and Italy.

By the end of the reign of the Emperor Augustus, Roman merchants had formed a number of guilds which had a virtual monopoly of traffic between Arles and Lyon, while others controlled the sea-going traffic from Arles to Rome. The guilds were rich and powerful, because the Roman Empire depended upon them for the supply of wheat, grown around Lyon and Narbonne, to Rome.

The Rhône near Chanaz, at the north end of Lac du Bourget

How did they cope with this violent river? By using the only limitless resource they had, manpower. The wheat and other produce was brought downstream in boats powered by sails and oars, like galleys. Taking goods upstream was another story. The boats had to be pulled against the current by huge gangs of slaves hauling on ropes attached to the boats.

Similar methods were used throughout the Middle Ages, but then, in addition to the dangers of the violent and capricious river, the merchants also had to face the brigandage of the lords who owned the land on either side. These petty princes ignored all royal authority, and when they did not actually plunder the cargoes being transported, they extorted heavy tolls

from all traffic. They also fought incessantly among themselves, and it was at the height of these disputes that the boats had the best chance of getting through safely.

The situation was so bad that when Louis IX travelled down the Rhône in 1248 to set sail from Aigues Mortes, leading the Eighth Crusade, he was so angered by reports of the piratical behaviour of the Lord of Chastel that he ordered his castle at La Roche de Glun, south of Tournon, to be completely destroyed.

The merchants were no better off when the lawless Middle Ages came to an end. Instead of paying 'protection money' to the war lords, they had to pay a toll to the various municipalities *en route*. There were 60 points

13

where a toll was payable, so that by the time a cargo taken on board at Lyon reached Arles its value had doubled.

The method of hauling the barges upstream by manpower continued until the 17th century. Then animals, either horses or oxen, were added to the teams, harnessed to ropes attached to a stout mast at the front of the boat. By the 19th century the barges were being drawn by teams of horses only. It was a specialised task in which the slightest mistake could result in the loss of men, horses or the boat itself. It took a team of 30 to 40 horses not less than a month to bring a fully laden barge from Arles to Lyon. The voyage downstream, aided by the fast current, and depending on the skill of the helmsman, was ten times quicker, only two or three days.

Despite the enormous difficulties, the traffic on the river was important. During the 18th and 19th centuries some hundreds of crews were at work. More than a thousand boats carried an average of 77,500 tons of goods up the Rhône every year, and more than 2,000 were used on the easier descent, carrying down about 142,000 tons annually, with half the boats returning empty. All this despite the fact that every year at least four months were lost, due either to high water drowning the towpaths completely, or to the water being so shallow that the risk of damage to the boats from running aground was too great. In an average year it was possible to make the voyage up the Rhône only eight times, and though the average time to Lyon

A dramatic view from one of the Haute Corniche belvederes in Ardèche

was one month, some voyages took much longer.

The teams which voyaged on the Rhône stopped every night. For centuries they supported a whole population of innkeepers, as well as ropemakers, ships' carpenters, blacksmiths, harness makers and the other artisans needed to repair the damage suffered by boats or their equipment through the hardships of the voyage.

The perils of the Rhône were such that no pilot would start a voyage without a prayer to St Nicholas for the safety of the boat and the crew. During the many days when navigation was not possible, the sailors would carve a mariner's cross. This could be as much as 1½m tall, and would be decorated with carvings of the instruments of the passion of Christ − nails, a hammer, a whip, a cockerel − as well as tools connected with the sailor's work, and might be topped with a representation of his particular boat. These crosses would be gaily painted and a large one would be mounted at the front of the leading boat, and each morning the captain would bless the cross with water from the river. Smaller examples of these crosses were made to decorate the sailors' own houses or for sale at ports along the river.

For 700 years the only bridges across the Rhône were those at Lyon at Pont-St Esprit, 200km to the south, and sometimes, when not washed away, at Avignon, 40km further south still. So it was not only the only north−south route but also, as it had always been, a barrier and a frontier between east and west.

This was the case when the brilliant engineer Marc Seguin began putting suspension bridges across the river in

1825. By 1850 there were eleven such bridges, and more were built by the end of the 19th century.

While the bridges were being built the haulage teams were still bringing barges up the river. But more important changes were taking place. Seguin altered the history of the river by inventing a steam boiler which was soon installed to provide power for steam-driven boats.

Early trials on the quiet river Saône were encouraging, and in 1827 M. Gaillard-Malezieux, a Lyon business-man, ordered the construction of a steam-driven boat 42m long. On 4 March crowds gathered on the banks of the river in the centre of Lyon to watch the trials of this new boat, intended for use on the Rhône. It was to travel 10km upstream from the Pont de la Guillotiere to a place called Le Pape, where the VIPs would disembark and enjoy a sumptuous celebratory lunch.

The *Rhône*, built by M. Derrheim of Calais, was the best-looking boat ever seen on the river. The hundreds of spectators watched in admiration as the black smoke poured from her funnels as she built up steam and began to move against the current, already at the start of the spring flood. Suddenly there was a great explosion, the boat disintegrated, and pieces of steel and wood began to rain down on the quaysides. Twenty-eight people were killed, including M. Gaillard-Malezieux and most of his associates, and many more were injured. It was suggested afterwards that the boilers had been made of steel of too thin a gauge in order to save weight, and that the engineers had blocked the safety valves in order to increase the steam pressure to enable the boat to fight against the current.

The effect of this tragic setback was short-lived. Only ten days later a new company was formed to build steamboats for use on the Rhône. Two years later, in 1829, the *Pioneer*, 75m long, made the first steam-powered voyage all the way from Lyon to Arles. It took only 14 hours and 25 minutes. The journey back took eight days, and in several places the boat had to be helped by teams of six horses. Even this tedious journey was still more than three times faster than previous ones and was enough to signal the slow death of horse-drawn traffic on the river.

By 1831 there were six steamers in regular service on the Rhône. The journey to Avignon, taking less than 14 hours, was a great deal quicker than the 38 hours of the stage coach, or the faster but uncomfortable journey by mail coach, and already the time for the return journey had been cut to 4½ days without the use of horses. By 1841 the number of steamboats carrying goods and passengers on the Rhône between Lyon and Arles had increased to 29, and they carried 76,000 tons of goods and 68,000 passengers in that year, but horse-drawn barges were still carrying more goods than that.

The river was already dangerous enough but in the 19th century it was soon found that it had become even more hazardous, because many of the new bridges had been built with arches that were much too low, so that when the river rose it was impossible for the boats to pass beneath them. It was realised as early as 1840 that at least five of the bridges between Lyon and Tournon ought to be raised. But only one, at Serrières, was altered, and the others repeatedly blocked the movement of traffic on the river.

In those days, before it was tamed by modern engineering, the current on the Rhône, even when not in flood, often reached 15k.p.h. Anyone watching a boat approaching the famous old bridge at Pont-St Esprit, with its 25 arches, would have been astonished to see being swept downstream broadside on and apparently out of control. It would have seemed inevitable that it would be smashed against one of the massive stone pillars, and such accidents did happen. But usually, at the very last moment, the front of the boat would be snatched around by the force of the current as it funnelled between the arches, and the boat would plunge through the centre of an arch like an arrow and shoot out on the other side. It required skill and nerve on the part of the sailors, and not a little courage on the part of passengers. The diarist John Evelyn, writing on 30 September 1644, said, 'The shooting of the Pont-St Esprit was attended by so much risk that timid passengers were often landed above the bridge and continued their journey by carriage.' Special pilots and special insurance rates were required for the passage through its sinister arches. In this respect the river was just as dangerous 250 years later.

Steam power meant that the haulage teams were gradually replaced by tugs and the tugs by self-propelled barges. The time taken for river voyages was reduced, but the river was still untamed and accidents were commonplace. Boats ran aground in unexpected shallows and crashed against the pillars of bridges, and in

1853 the *Parisien* exploded as the *Rhône* had done, and for the same reason. Six people were killed. Disasters were not confined to boats. Bridges were carried away by floods, and even blown down by the mistral. The flood of 1840 smashed the bridges of Vienne and Teil, flooded the centre of Lyon, and swamped 90 per cent of the houses in Avignon. There were further terrible floods in 1856, 1896, 1910 and 1928.

The development of the railways took more and more goods traffic from the river, and with their arrival the dominance of the Rhône as a transport route was over. But the latest floods made people realise that something had to be done to discipline the river, and in 1933 a company was formed, the Compagnie Nationale du Rhône, with the object of harnessing its great power for useful purposes. The job it undertook was the development of the river from the Swiss frontier to the Mediterranean, from 'the triple point of view of hydroelectricity, navigation, and irrigation. . . .'

The work began with the construction of a new port at Lyon. Then in 1937 the first barrage was built, at Génissiat between Lyon and Geneva. Since then 23 hydroelectric projects and other engineering works have been constructed on the river. The Rhône has been made into a huge water staircase between Lyon and the sea.

The gigantic size of the works undertaken is understood best by what was done near Montélimar, at Donzère-Mondragon. At the outlet of the Donzère gorge part of the waters of the Rhône were diverted into a new canal 28km long, 145m wide and 10m deep. The hydroelectric station

17

at Bollène, 17km down the canal, uses the flow, which can be controlled by valves plus a maximum fall of 23m, and produces about one-thirtieth of all French hydroelectric power. Some water flows continuously through the natural river bed, and more is allowed through when the river rises, so that flooding can be controlled. The Donzère-Mondragon works included two new railway bridges and eight new road bridges.

The river produces more than 16,000 million kWh of electricity, more than one-twentieth of all French consumption, and, in simple terms, it is this which is paying the astronomical cost of all the works on the Rhône.

Secondary benefits include the permanent irrigation of more than 200,000ha of fertile land, safer navigation on long stretches of the river, and the prevention of the flooding of thousands of hectares.

But the Rhône is not now a demure old lady of a river. It does not, like the Thames, run softly. At times it can still be dangerous. This is what Gerard Morgan Grenfell had to say in his book *Barging into Southern France* about leaving Lyon by the Pierre Benite lock, with his barge in the hands of an experienced river pilot.

After the lock cut of Pierre Benite we re-entered the river and almost at once there was a swirling and a surface bubbling of a kind I had never before seen. From one side to the other there were little whirlpools and sudden unaccountable waves. Small pieces of driftwood bobbing along the surface would suddenly disappear, as though pulled beneath by an invisible hand. Wherever there was a solid object breaking the surface, a rock, or a concrete pier, the water would be piled up against one side and hollowed out on the other in a manner which could hardly fail to impress the mariner. Due to the river's width the sensation of speed was not apparent except where we drew near to the bank. Our course criss-crossed the river repeatedly and not always in the manner indicated on the chart. At first I attributed this to lack of knowledge on the part of the pilot, or to there being no need to follow the dotted line with any accuracy. I remained suspicious until, right in the middle of the indicated path, I saw a yacht tilted and evidently holed in water that must have been shallow indeed.... The wind was rising appreciably whipping the surface into small dark waves. The scenery passed by with improbable speed. The problems we were experiencing were no doubt petty compared to those formerly experienced by the horse-drawn traffic which defied the powerful Rhône currents between Lyon and Arles.

This was written after, not before, the engineering works in the Lyon area had been completed.

3
Food and Wine

There is no doubt that Lyon is the gastronomic capital of the western world. It was here that cookery became established as an art. In 1825, Brillat Savarin, who came from Belley, near Lyor, in the upper Rhône Valley, produced his classic book *The Physiology of Taste*. Then came Lucién Tendret, also from Belley, who wrote a lyrical masterpiece on the art of cooking in the Lyonnais. The famous writer, Stendhal, was another enthusiast for Lyon cooking, which he described in his book 'Memoires of a Tourist' in 1838, as much better than that of Paris. A hundred years later, Curnonsky, elected by 3,000 gourmets as the Prince of Gastronomes, called Lyon the world capital of gastronomy.

Nowhere else are the heights of the culinary arts reached as often as they are here. From Fernand Point onwards a succession of brilliant chefs have set the highest standards throughout the region. Today Paul Bocuse, Gerard Nandron, Jean Vettard, Pierre Orsi, Roger Roucou, Philippe Chavent, Jean-Paul Lacombe and Christian Bourillot, lead the way in and around Lyon. They are matched by master chefs in other towns of the region: Georges Blanc at Vonnas, Jacques Pic at Valence and Guy Thivard at Vienne.

Meals in such restaurants can never be cheap. Bocuse employs 50 people to maintain his standards, and has to charge the best part of 200 francs just to cover his costs. Great as they are, these chefs still go to market themselves, still seek the best, still look for improvement. Every Monday at the Café du Marché in Lyon, chefs meet to discuss their art and exchange ideas.

Apart from its chefs, the supremacy of Lyon is due to two things. First, there is the unequalled supply of superb raw materials: fish from the mountain lakes and rivers of Savoy and Isère; poultry from the Bresse region; beef from the Charollais; lamb from Drôme and Isère; game of all kinds from Les Dombes and Savoy; local cheeses in great variety; fruit and vegetables of the highest quality from the Rhône Valley; and added to all this, the choice of the superb wines of Burgundy, Beaujolais, and the Côtes du Rhône, all within easy reach. Secondly, there is the relentless enthusiasm of the people of the region for good food, and their knowledge and vigilance in ensuring that standards are maintained.

Another dimension is added to the Lyonnais cooking by the famous *Mères*. These women chefs and restaurateurs

A shop selling the nougat for which Montélimar is famous

give their own feminine touch to *haute cuisine*. Perhaps the best-known of them today is Mère Brazier, who is the third generation to keep the famous restaurant of this name. While the best male chefs are often innovative, the Mères tend to keep to well-tried recipes and reproduce them at a constant high standard.

The large and discerning public and the many restaurants mean that competition is intense in Lyon at all levels. In practice this means that you can be confident of getting good value for money in the simplest bistro in Lyon, while for gourmets the great restaurants provide meals which are the stuff of legend. Some of the local specialities are Partridge in Chartreuse, Saddle of Hare in Cream Sauce,

Chicken Liver Pie, Gratin of Crayfish Tails, Quenelles of Pike and Braised Stuff Trout. There are many others.

The Savoy region has its own specialities of which the best known is Fondue Savoyarde, a traditional alpine delicacy made by melting Gruyère cheese in dry white wine. Once melted the fondue is kept creamy on a small spirit stove or other low heat, and half a glass of kirsch is stirred into it. It is eaten from cubes of dried bread dipped into it on long forks. The wines of Savoy, both red and white, are very drinkable, particularly the fruity whites.

In the northern part of the Rhône Valley butter is used in cooking, but in Provence, southern Drôme and southern Ardèche, the cooking is based on olive oil, and, as the raw

20

materials are less varied and of lesser quality, more herbs and spices are used to heighten the flavour. A good deal less meat is eaten in Provence than further north and many dishes are based on vegetables. It is only on the coast that fish and shellfish are much eaten, and then mostly on high days and holidays. Typical Provençal dishes include Soupe au Pistou, made with fresh vegetables and a thick sauce of garlic, tomatoes, basil (*pistou*) and olive oil; bouillabaisse, a stew of rock fish such as gurnard, scorpion fish, angler fish, red mullet, and bass, among others. The broth and the fish should be served separately but not all restaurants do this. Bourride is a similar dish, except that it is prepared from white fish such as turbot, grey mullet, bass, etc. It is often served with aioli, a thick paste of creamed garlic, yolk of egg and olive oil, which can be stirred into the broth of the fish soup and eaten on bread.

The full-bodied wines of the southern Rhône Valley are better with the more highly flavoured Provençal dishes than the lighter and more delicately flavoured wines of the more northern vineyards.

In deference to tourist tastes, most Provençal restaurants these days offer a Salade Niçoise which contains lettuce and tuna fish, but you may come across the real thing in some out of the way places, made from tomatoes, artichokes, beans, green pepper, cucumber, raw onions, garlic, black

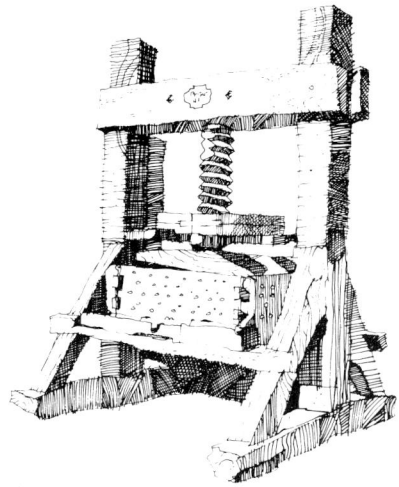

A 16th-century wine-press at Châteauneuf-du-Pape

olives, anchovy fillets and hard-boiled eggs. Another popular local dish is ratatouille, a mixture of vegetables including onions, tomatoes, courgettes, red and green peppers and aubergines, cooked together in olive oil, and served hot or cold.

It is a good idea to eat meals based on local produce — that is what they know how to prepare best of all. In hotels and restaurants open all year, it will be safe and economical to take the 'house' wine. In seasonal, tourist restaurants it is not such a good idea, and it is better to take a bottle of local wine or something you know.

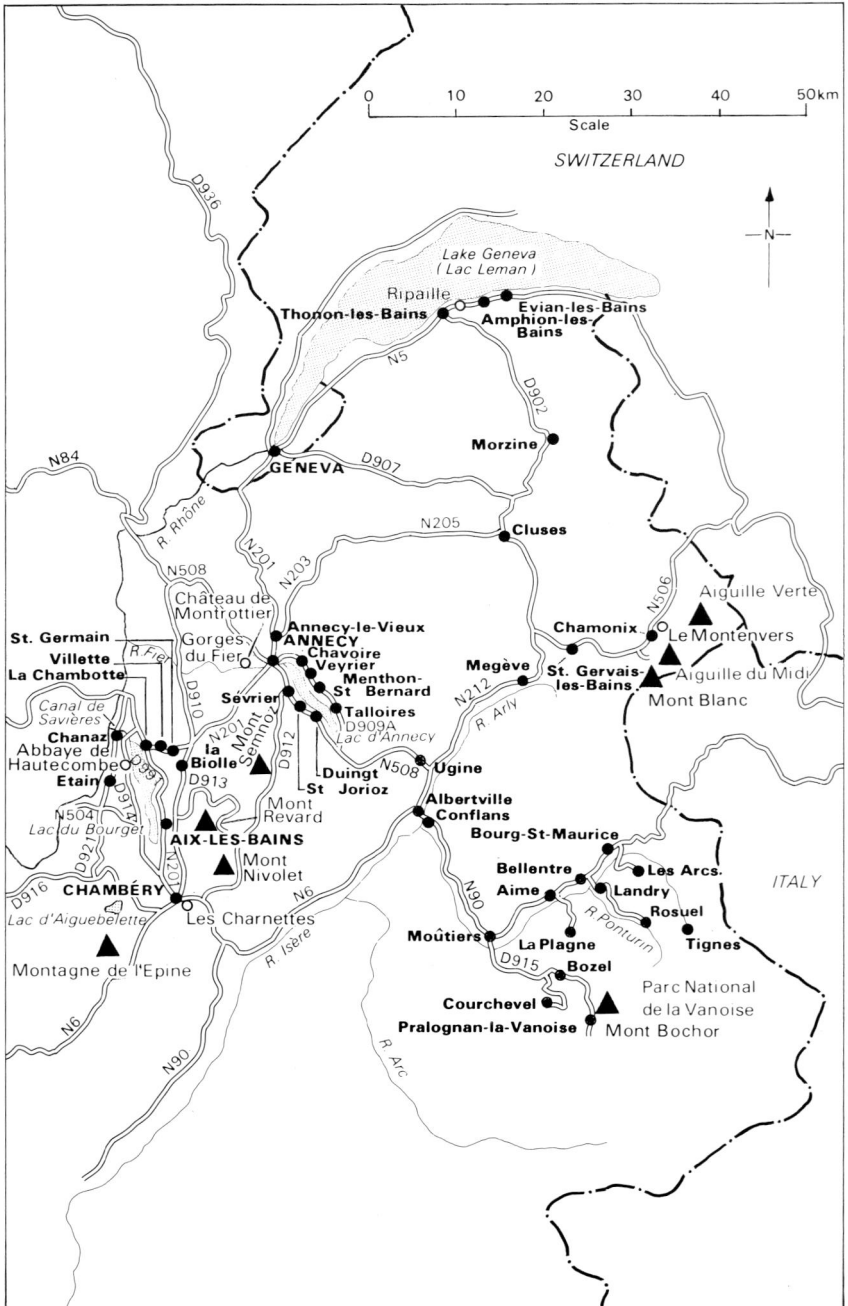

0   10   20   30   40   50km

Scale

SWITZERLAND

—N—

Lake Geneva
(Lac Leman)

Ripaille

Evian-les-Bains

Thonon-les-Bains

Amphion-les-Bains

D936

D916

N5

Morzine

D902

GENEVA

N84

D907

R Rhône

N205

Cluses

N508

N201

N203

N506

Aiguille Verte

Château de Montrottier

Chamonix

Le Montenvers

Gorges du Fier

St. Germain

Annecy-le-Vieux

ANNECY

Chavoire

Veyrier

Megève

St. Gervais-les-Bains

Aiguille du Midi

Villette

La Chambotte

R Fier

Menthon-St Bernard

N212

R Arly

Mont Blanc

Sevrier

Talloires

Canal de Savières

D910

D912

D909A

Lac d'Annecy

Chanaz

N201

la Biolle

Duingt

St Jorioz

N508

Ugine

ITALY

Abbaye de Hautecombe

D921

D913

Mont Semnoz

Etain

Mont Revard

Albertville

Conflans

N504

Lac du Bourget

AIX-LES-BAINS

Mont Nivolet

Bourg-St-Maurice

Bellentre

Les Arcs

D916

D921

CHAMBÉRY

N6

Aime

Landry

N201

Rosuel

Lac d'Aiguebelette

Les Charnettes

Moûtiers

R Ponturin

Tignes

Montagne de l'Epine

R Isère

N90

La Plagne

D915

Bozel

Courchevel

Parc National de la Vanoise

Pralognan-la-Vanoise

Mont Bochor

R Arc

N6

N90

22

4
Savoy

Though it switches from bank to bank to describe the delightful country on either side, this guide essentially follows the Rhône downstream from its entry into France from Switzerland all the way to the Mediterranean.

As it begins its journey through France, it forms the northern boundary of the old Principality of Savoy, which, as far as modern France is concerned, means the departments of Haute Savoie and Savoie. Together they form a region of unmatched scenic beauty, a labyrinth of grandiose mountain peaks enclosing deep valleys with green pastures and pine-clad upper slopes, of torrents and rivers, and alpine lakes big and small. It is a landscape which both soothes and inspires the human spirit.

For a remote, cut-off, poor and largely infertile region Savoy has had a curious and significant history. It began when Humbert of the White Hands, lord of the Alpine valley of Maurienne, was made Count of Savoy in 1034, in return for military services rendered to Conrad, then ruler of the Holy Roman Empire. This action founded a state and a royal house which was to last for nearly 1,000 years, ending only when Umberto II, the last King of Italy, abdicated in 1946.

In the 14th century the size and importance of Savoy were considerably increased by the efforts of three energetic rulers in succession. Amédée VI, a formidable horseman, known as the Green Count from the colour of his tunic when jousting, extended Savoy towards Switzerland, the Jura, and Italy. Amédée VII, known as the Red Count, because in battle his armour was always covered in blood, added the Comté of Nice to Savoy. Amédée VIII was made a duke by the Emperor Sigismond, and further enlarged Savoy by adding the area around Geneva and the much larger province of Piedmont, on the Italian side of the Alps from Savoy.

In 1536, François I of France attacked Savoy, which he saw as a stepping stone in the furtherance of his ambition to dominate Italy. For 23 years Savoy remained under the control of France, until Henri II signed the Treaty of Cateau Cambresis in 1559, by which the Duke of Savoy regained his state. He at once moved his capital further away from France, from Chambéry to Turin in Piedmont.

The destiny of the ruling house of Savoy was changed by the Treaty of Utrecht in 1713, which settled the complicated political issues of the War of the Spanish Succession. Under the terms of the treaty Victor Amédée of Savoy became King of Sicily. Five years later he swapped Sicily for Sardinia. From that time Savoy and Sardinia were known as the Sardinian States, or the Kingdom of Sardinia.

Savoy was still coveted by France, and during the French Revolution it was successfully attacked by French troops. It became part of France and was named the department of Mont Blanc. This situation continued until the Treaty of Paris in 1815, when Savoy was returned to King Victor Emmanuel I. The House of Savoy remained rulers of Sardinia and Piedmont, and as the unification of Italy became an important issue in the middle of the 19th century, they realised that they would have the best claim to rule the whole of Italy. But first they had to get rid of the Austrians, who were attacking the north. They appealed for help to Napoleon III of France who sent troops to join them in driving the Austrians out of Italy. In return for this assistance Savoy and Nice were ceded to France in 1860. Ten years later King Victor Emmanuel II became the first king of a united Italy. The ambitions of the House of Savoy had been achieved, but when Umberto II gave up the throne in 1946 their power came to an end.

In the past Savoy was considered a poor region, where the living was hard, and where the people were rough in manners and lacking in culture, and often suffered from goitres from drinking snow water. In the late 19th century that was about all that the rest of France knew about Savoy. But first alpinism and then tourism have changed all that. The lovely lakes in their spectacular mountain settings, and the vast snowfields with their gentle slopes among peaks crowned by the majesty of Mont Blanc, have in recent years made Savoy an important holiday destination. There are now about 100 ski resorts in Savoy, 40 of them of international standard, making the area one of the most popular destinations for both alpine and cross-country skiing.

But there is more to Savoy than winter sports. It has also become a summer holiday destination. Aix-les-Bains is the second most popular spa in France, and there are six more in Savoy. Annecy is one of the finest lakeside resorts in Europe and there are other attractive places around the shores of its beautiful lake. In summer the Lac d'Annecy and the Lac du Bourget, the largest natural lake in France, become centres of yachting, and there are many smaller lakes popular with canoeists, windsurfers, and anglers.

In summer, from the valley slopes to high up the mountainsides, Savoy becomes a region to explore at leisure, by car or on foot, on horseback, or by bicycle along hundreds of kilometres of signposted paths, including some of the national footpaths, the Grandes Randonnées, and always with the varied background of the mountains, constantly changing as the sun moves round. There are five nature reserves in Savoy, as well as the 53,000ha Vanoise National Park, a natural paradise of forests, glaciers, alpine meadows and mountain springs.

From the valley of the Rhône in the north the land rises steadily towards the Lac d'Annecy and the Lac de Bourget at the foot of the Savoy Alps.

Annecy (pop. 52,000) is an excellent base from which to explore the area. It is the prefecture of Haute

Savoie, and a good example of what the tourist industry can do for a place. It was poor. It is prosperous. It was small. It is five times as big today as it was 100 years ago. It is not really a town to visit for its architectural or historical interest. There are no great churches or cathedrals, the castle is not particularly impressive, and there is not much in the way of museums. But what Annecy lacks on the cultural side, it more than makes up for in charm. The town has made the most of its lovely situation. The well-laid-out parks and gardens which border the lake have magnificent views of the surrounding mountains. Swans and other waterfowl glide on tree-lined canals and beside flower-decked waterside promenades. More flowers line the banks and the ancient bridges of the river Thiou which flows through the old quarter. Renaissance houses and pleasant café-restaurants line the quays.

Tourists arriving by car in Annecy should make for the Parking Bonlieu in the centre of town, near the lake. This is a spacious underground car park beneath the Maison de Tourisme, a modern building which includes shops and offices and a new theatre, as well as the Tourist Office. There is also a café where light meals can be obtained, though most visitors may prefer to try one of the restaurants in the old town. The lakeside park, the old quarter and the canals around the river Thiou are all within a short walk of the Maison de Tourisme.

Annecy is an ideal spot for a relaxed holiday, just taking your ease and enjoying the wonderful scenery. For those who want exercise there are 24 tennis courts, an 18-hole golf course where players enjoy panoramic views,

riding stables, swimming pools, and lakeside beaches. Boats of all kinds are available for trips on the lake, which is about 15km long and up to 4km wide. It is worth taking the 1½-hour boat trip round the lake, just for the variety of the mountain scenery, which looks its best in the afternoon and towards evening. Some of the boats are quite large, and one, called La Libellule (The Dragonfly) does regular dinner cruises on summer evenings and has room for 630 diners.

The old quarter of Annecy, la vieille ville, should not be confused with **Annecy-le-Vieux** which is a separate place on the outskirts of Annecy about 2km to the north. It is famous for the Paccard bell foundry, whose church bells ring all over the world. The most famous of the countless bells made here since the firm was founded in 1796 is the 'Savoyarde'. It is the largest bell in the world that can be swung, and was made for the Sacré-Coeur in Paris in 1891. The clapper weighs nearly a ton, and the bell itself almost 19 tons. There is an interesting and unusual museum devoted to all aspects of campanology and the making of bells.

One can easily make a complete tour round the Lac d'Annecy by car. It links a number of picturesque villages and offers a succession of beautiful lake and mountain views, better, as one tourist was heard to say, than any chocolate box! Take the N508 south from Annecy and immediately beside the lake to Sevrier. Here you can either continue on the same road beside the lake to St Jorioz and Duingt, or turn right on to the D912 which climbs up and along the side of the Semnoz mountain. After only about 2km there is a belvedere with splendid views

Lac d'Annecy viewed from the Jardin Public in Annecy town

over the lake. A little further on a narrow road on the left leads steeply down to St Jorioz where you can rejoin the main road towards Duingt. (The D912 continues into the mountains and away from the lake.)

Duingt is a village of typical Savoyard houses, with outside staircases and red-tiled roofs. It is situated on a promontory at the narrowest part of the lake, with a view across to Talloires. At the extreme end of the promontory is the romantic looking Château de Duingt with its turrets and round tower reflected in the clear water.

The Thiou Canal which flows through the charming old town centre of Annecy

About 2km beyond the end of the lake a left turn, the D909A, leads back along the other side of the shore to Talloires. This elegant little resort has one of the best restaurants in France, L'Auberge du Père Bise.

A few kilometres further on from Talloires is **Menthon-St Bernard**, the birthplace of St Bernard de Menthon who gave his name to the Great St Bernard and Little St Bernard passes and, of course, the dog, and founded hospices for mountain travellers. As the present towered and turreted castle has no part older than the 12th century, the room shown to tourists as the birthplace of St Bernard in the 10th century must come under the heading of touristic licence. The château, which is mostly 14th- and 15th-century

27

There are beautiful lake views from Talloires

well restored in the 19th, is worth a visit. The most surprising thing about it is that, since its origin in the 12th century it has been in the hands of the same family, the Menthons.

The mountains rise steeply from this side of the lake with the road and the villages tucked tightly between them and the water. Almost the only exception is between Talloires and Menthon-St Bernard where, on the left of the road, the small plateau of Roc de Chère holds one of the world's most superbly sited golf courses. From Menthon-St Bernard return to Annecy through Veyrier and Chavoire.

Another worthwhile short excursion from Annecy is to the Gorges du Fier and the Château de Montrottier. The river Fier pours through a narrow,

rocky cleft more than 60m deep. The special interest for the visitor is that a safe iron gangway runs for 250m along the face of the sheer rock wall. A stroll along this gangway with the river raging and roaring only 20m below, with the sky only a crack above the dark and sinister gorge, is a good reminder of the savagery that nature can let loose. Halfway along there is a scale showing the heights reached by the river in flood, including September 1960, when it rose 27m above its normal level.

The **Château de Montrottier** stands near the bridge across the gorge. It is a 13th–16th-century castle with a 36m high keep, built in 1427, within the walls. At different periods the château belonged to the princes of Savoy, then

The château at Menthon-St Bernard, on the shores of Lac d'Annecy

to the Menthon family, and then others. The last owner, a rich collector of antiques left it to the state, together with an interesting collection of arms and armour, period furniture, tapestries and wooden carvings. It is open to the public for guided visits, morning and afternoon, from Palm Sunday to mid-October; closed on Tuesdays except from June to mid-September.

Evian-les-Bains is a place which most guidebooks miss, probably because it is tucked away in a remote corner of France, but I include it for two reasons. First, it is not very far from Annecy and the trip makes a good day's excursion by car, especially for those who want to see Lake Geneva (Lac Leman), 15 times larger than the Lac d'Annecy. Secondly, it is beautifully situated between the lakeshore and the foothills of the Chablais moun-

tains, and is a comfortable, well-laid-out and well-appointed place. The best route from Annecy follows the N203, then N205 to Cluses, and then the D902 to Thonon-les-Bains, which is linked to Evian by the N5.

As long ago as the 1890s, when its population was less than 3,000, it was already a small resort popular with fashionable French society. The casino, the old thermal establishment and one or two big villas, with their imposing turn-of-the-century architecture, are reminders of those times. Although it has about doubled in size in the past 100 years and has every kind of modern amenity, Evian remains a small and rather exclusive resort.

There is a harbour where boats arrive and depart for trips on the lake, and two yacht marinas, as well as a beach area with a large open-air swimming pool. The new spa buildings are in a pleasant park opposite the port, and are open from 1 March to Christmas Day. The famous Evian water is used in the spa to treat kidney and digestive disorders. The former pump room of the old thermal establishment, where visitors taking the waters used to drink from the Cachat spring, named after the first man to exploit them, is an attractive Art Nouveau pavilion holding a small exhibition concerning Evian water. A modern factory, which can be visited, at Amphion-les-Bains, 3km along the coast road from Evian, bottles the water for sale all over the world. Amphion is a pleasant little resort, no longer a spa although it was the first in the region and was used by the princes of Savoy in the 17th century.

Thonon-les-Bains, along the coast from Evian and Amphion, and on the main route to and from Annecy, is a much bigger town, and a sous-prefecture of Haute Savoie. It has some very good viewpoints over Lake Geneva from the Jardin Anglais and the gardens around the place du Château.

There is not much of historical interest in these lakeside resorts but 2km outside Thonon-les-Bains the **Domaine de la Ripaille** is worth a visit. At the beginning of the 14th century there was nothing here but a lakeside forest used by the lords of Savoy as a hunting ground. But towards the end of the 14th century Bonne de Bourbon, wife of the Green Count, Amédée VI, had a country house built here. Nothing much remains of this because her grandson, Amédée VIII, while at the height of his power, suddenly abdicated and handed over to his son. He retired to Ripaille where he built a

château and founded the monastic order of St Maurice with six of his knights. He was as respected as a holy man as he had been as a ruler, and in 1439 he was elected Pope, or rather anti-Pope, because although the great split in the Catholic Church which had resulted in two popes, one in Avignon and one in Rome had officially ended in 1417, the differences in fact continued, and at one time there were even three popes. Amédée, who as Pope was known as Felix V, tried for ten years to gain recognition among the great nations of Europe, but then gave up the papacy and retired to his monastery at Ripaille, where he remained a monk until he died. The monastic order of St Maurice came to an end after his death.

The château is an attractive building, very Savoyard in style. The interior was restored at the turn of this century in the neo-Gothic style in fashion at the time. Today the château is the headquarters of the Ripaille Foundation, which concerns itself with ecology, geography, and the development of natural resources. The château is open to the public for guided visits, morning and afternoon, from June to the end of September. There is also an extensive arboretum open to the public, with a choice of one- or two-hour routes (signposted).

Albertville lies 45km from Annecy via the N508 to Ugine and then the N212. It is situated at the confluence of the Isère and the Arly, and is a 19th-century creation. In 1835 Charles Albert, King of Savoy and Sardinia, decreed that the old town of Conflans, on a hill above the river, should be united with the quarter called L'Hopital at the riverside, and that the new community should be called

Albertville. Now a smart modern town, the centre for the 1992 Winter Olympics, it is well kept and has plenty of flowers about, but is a place of no special interest. Conflans, however, retains its own identity up on the hill and merits a visit.

Once a busy little market town **Conflans** has long been passed by, but not entirely. Its narrow streets, its graceful arcades, its old towers, have attracted modern craftsmen, painters, potters, woodcarvers and others who have made the medieval shops along the old high street their studios. The moment you walk through the postern gate a curious thing strikes you – much of Conflans is built of reddish-brown brick, something rare in Savoy. Nobody knows the when or why of this, though the Maison Rouge, which now houses the municipal museum, is 14th-century and Florentine in style, and the Château Rouge, once a residence of the princes of Savoy, resembles a small Venetian palace.

The early 18th-century church has a typically bulbous Savoyard steeple. The interior is not of special interest except that it has a very unusual pulpit carved in Baroque style by the sculptor Jacques Clerans in 1718.

Conflans is the kind of place where you can saunter at will and find something every few yards to evoke your interest or admiration. There is an 18th-century fountain in the Grande Place, and from the place de la Grande Roche there are views across the valley to the mountain panorama beyond.

Chamonix, 67km from Albertville via the N212 and N506, bases its claim to be the world capital of alpinism on its famous Company of Guides, a kind of combined union and school for guides, founded in 1821. Others have

followed since but that of Chamonix remains *the* company. It is also a centre for all the accessories of modern mountain climbing, such as the ice axes which have been made by four generations of the Moser family and are known to climbers all over the world. The approach to Chamonix along the valley of the Arve offers some magnificent views of the Mont Blanc Massif.

Of the many excursions into the mountains available to non-climbers from Chamonix, that to the summit of the Aiguille du Midi must rank as one of the world's greatest tourist experiences. It takes you up to over 3,800m and it is important to take warm clothes and sunglasses, and not to make any physical effort near the summit. The trip, by cable car and lift, takes at least two hours, including an intermediate stop and time at the top.

Though not so high, 2,500m, the excursion to the summit of Le Brevent, by cable car, is well worthwhile. It is further from Mont Blanc and offers perhaps the finest view of all of the whole Massif, including the Aiguille du Midi.

Another famous excursion is the one to see the Sea of Ice from Montenvers, at 1,913m. This trip is made by cog railway. There is an impressive view across the glacier of the Sea of Ice to the Aiguille Dru and the Aiguille Verte, with the great wall of the Grandes Jorasses mountains as backcloth.

Mont Blanc dominates the Alps by reason of its height but for my taste, as a spectacle the Aiguille Verte is a more impressive sight. Because it is more detached, its shape, which is both elegant and rugged, seems more

Mont Blanc

The pride of Savoy is Mont Blanc, the highest mountain in Europe, and the headquarters of the Mont Blanc area and of alpinism is the little town of Chamonix. Today Chamonix is also a fully equipped summer resort with sporting facilities of all kinds, including an 18 hole golf course, tennis, swimming pools, covered skating rink, and summer skiing.

There is a very interesting alpine museum which illustrates the history of the valley of Chamonix, unknown to the outside world until it was explored by two young Englishmen, Windham and Pocock, in 1741. It also illustrates the development of mountain climbing, the changes in costume and equipment over the years, and contains documents and photographs of famous ascents. Exhibits include the ice axe involved in Captain Arkwright's fatal fall in 1866. Thirty years later parts of Arkwright's body and clothes emerged at the face of the glacier des Bossons, having been transported by the ice 2,000 metres down from the site of the accident.

The summer before Arkwright's accident, the greatest alpinist of them all, Edward Whymper, had made the first successful ascent of the Matterhorn. He climbed it with three companions and three guides. On the way down triumph turned to tragedy. One of the party slipped, dragging three others with him. The rope broke and the four of them hurtled to their deaths. Only Whymper and two of the guides survived. Whymper was deeply affected by the disaster, and never climbed in the Alps again. He made some great ascents in the Andes, and wrote books about Chamonix and Zermatt. He died in Chamonix in 1911, aged 71. Both he and Arkwright are buried in the Anglican cemetery there.

The tunnel

The Mont Blanc tunnel, linking France to Italy, takes about half an hour to drive through at the recommended maximum speed of 70km per hour where this is possible. It has two lanes, each 7m wide plus a pavement for emergency use by pedestrians in the event of a breakdown. There are emergency stopping places for cars every 300m and refuges for pedestrians every 100m. The tunnel is banned to ordinary pedestrians, and overtaking and voluntary stopping of cars is forbidden.

When it was built thirty years ago (from 1959 to 1965) it was the longest road tunnel in the world, but there are now three others in the Alps that are longer, the St Gothard, Arlberg, and Fréjus. At the deepest point, beneath the Aiguille du Midi, there are 2,480m of rock above the tunnel. On the French side the tunnel starts near Chamonix at the hamlet of Les Pélérins, 1,274m. In the 11.5km of its length it climbs about 100m to the hamlet of Entrèves on the Italian side. The ventilation system draws in 900m^3 of fresh air every second, enough for 450 vehicles an hour to use the tunnel.

majestic. There is another very fine view of this mountain from La Flégère, 1,894m, also accessible by cable car.

In addition to these excursions it is also possible to make a complete tour of the Mont Blanc Massif by car, a distance of about 320km. To get the best out of this trip you should travel in very leisurely fashion, with stops to enjoy the views and take photographs. If you like, overnight stops can be made in Martigny in Switzerland, or Courmayeur or Aosta in Italy. For those mountain lovers who are experienced walkers there is a signposted footpath which circumnavigates the whole of the Massif, passing through Switzerland and Italy and back into Savoy. This walking tour normally takes 8–10 days, and if you want a guide, you can hire one who knows every peak visible on the route. There are, of course, many shorter walks along signposted footpaths on the lower slopes of Mont Blanc.

Megève, which lies on the N212 about halfway between Albertville and Chamonix, is one of France's most successful and steadily fashionable alpine resorts. It first made its reputation as a health resort, after the First World War, becoming well known for its sunny and bracing climate. Then in the 1930s it became *the* winter-sports resort. It has one of the world's most important ski schools, and also a rock-climbing school. Its comfortable hotels, good restaurants, and all-year sports facilities which include riding, tennis, and swimming, have ensured its popularity without losing its smart clientele. It has particularly good facilities for children.

Another wonderful mountain area, but of a different kind, is the great national park in the south-east corner

of Savoy. Whereas the Mont Blanc area has every modern and technical device of tourism to enable visitors to enjoy the mountains with a minimum of effort, nothing of the kind exists in the **Parc National de la Vanoise**. It was established in 1963 with the specific purpose of keeping a large area of the Alps in their natural state, entirely untouched by and protected from the inroads of tourism. The only concession was to the safety of those visitors who venture there, by the establishment of 29 mountain refuges, anything from two to nine hours' walk from each other.

This huge national park covers nearly 53,000ha and is united across a long section of the border with the Italian national park of Gran Paradis. Together they form one of the few places in Europe where nature remains as it was, untouched by man. When you enter this world of glaciers, mountain peaks, and crystal torrents, you leave your car, comfort, and the 20th century at the gate. You can nevertheless enjoy all that the park offers in perfect safety. In this area there are 107 peaks more than 3,000m high, but there are also valleys with larch woods and green slopes covered with a variety of alpine flowers, and natural rock gardens. Yellow anemones, pink azaleas, purple and pink Martagon lilies, white and yellow buttercups, and more rarely edelweiss, are just some of the flowers. There is also a rich animal life. The ibex is rare in Europe but here there are about a thousand, as well as about five thousand chamois, on the French side. The squirrel-like marmot, which lives underground and hibernates in winter, is common and there are hares of various kinds, as well as foxes, badgers,

An ibex: you may be lucky enough to see a wild one in the mountains of Savoy

and mountain voles. The park is home to birds of several species, from the little alpine sparrow to the majestic eagle. But the wildlife of the park is not accustomed to people and distances itself from them, so it is essential to have a good pair of binoculars with you.

The best time to visit the park is towards the end of June, when the days are long, the flowers are at their best and there are fewer people about. The easiest approaches are the N90 and D915 from Albertville via Moutiers and Bozel, and then continue along the D915 to Pralognan-la-Vanoise, or via Moutiers and then the N90 to Aime and Bellentre, and then Landry and up the valley of the Ponturin to the refuge at Rosuel and the gate of the park. From both these starting

points there are attractive walks into the park.

Travel inside the park must be on foot, skis or horseback. There are 500km of signposted footpaths which are open from 1 June to the end of September. Anyone seriously considering walking in the park should obtain the Topoguide of the GR5 and the GR55, walking maps available from good map shops in Britain, but hard to find in France where stocks are soon exhausted. Note should be taken of the practical advice contained in these specialist guides.

From Rosuel it is a 2½-hour climb, mostly following the GR5 to the small Lac de la Plagne, with a descent of about 1¾ hours. From the lake it is possible to continue to the Col du Palet, 2,653m, with superb mountain views. This adds another four hours of walking there and back, making a full day for the whole walk. There is a guarded refuge at the Col.

From Pralognan there is a 3-hour return walk to Mont Bochor, or you can reach the summit by cable car in six minutes, and from there start the three-hour walk along the GR55 to the Col de la Vanoise where there is another guarded refuge. Less ambitious walkers can take the car along a mountain road from Pralognan to the La Chollière hill, park it and then wander, to enjoy the views, and the wild narcissus and gentian and other flowers in the surrounding meadows.

All serious mountain walks should be undertaken only by fit and experienced ramblers equipped with stout, non-slip boots or shoes. In mountains the length of time required for a walk is calculated not so much by distance as by the change of level involved. Going up is calculated at about 300m per hour and coming down at about 500m per hour. All mountain walks should be started early in the morning, and those mentioned here enable walkers to return to base on the same day, though it is possible to overnight in one of the refuges, which offer couchette accommodation. Details of guided walks are available in the resorts around the park, including La Plagne, Les Arcs, and Tignes, the highest ski resort in France, where skiing is possible every day of the year.

Chambéry, the prefecture of the department of Savoie is about 50km south of Annecy, about 50km west of Albertville via the N90, and only 15km south of Aix-les-Bains. From 1232 until 1562 it was the capital of the state of Savoy, and the castle there was the chief residence of the rulers, the princely family who eventually became kings of Italy.

Today Chambéry is an administrative and commercial centre for a wide region. Its expansion over recent years is obvious from the number of modern buildings and tall office blocks, but it still has an interesting old quarter which has been well restored and is worth a look round. You can begin at the Elephant Fountain, a sort of mascot with the inhabitants of Chambéry. More of a curiosity than a work of art, it was erected to the memory of General Count de Boigne who had made a fortune in India and had been a generous benefactor to the town. The water from the fountain flows down the trunks of the four elephants, who stand back to back in pairs. The monument, a reminder of the general's association with India, is always known to the locals as the *quatre sans culs* or just the *sans culs*,

a phrase which translates politely as the 'no backsides' or 'no behinds', as only the front half of each elephant is seen.

Walk down the rue Ducis and turn right into the rue de la Croix d'Or which has a number of fine 17th- and 18th-century mansions. Plaques fixed to the houses give basic dates and details. Turn right into the pleasant place St Leger, which was restored, repaved and turned into a pedestrian precinct in the 1970s. There are several lively cafés where the Chambériens like to watch the world go by.

The château, the former residence of the dukes and princes of Savoy, is of medieval origin but has been considerably altered and rebuilt over the centuries, first in the 14th and 15th, and has been partly burned down and rebuilt twice more since then. But some points of interest remain. There are guided tours. The Sainte Chapelle, in the castle complex, is a fine example of the Flamboyant Gothic style, except that the façade was reconstructed in Baroque style in the 17th century. It was named the Sainte Chapelle when the supposed shroud of Christ was deposited there in 1456 (it was moved to Turin in 1578). There are three large and very fine stained-glass windows in the apse.

Many of the streets in the old town are linked by covered passages between the houses, called *allées*. Return to the Elephant Fountain via the rue de Juiverie and the rue de Boigne.

Chambéry's Museum of Fine Arts has a very good collection of Italian paintings of all periods. It includes a superb 'Portrait of a Young Man' usually attributed to Paolo Uccello, but believed by the great critic Berenson to be the work of Masaccio.

The unusual Elephant Fountain in Chambéry

About 2km outside Chambéry is Les Charmettes, a small country house, originally 18th-century, with a pointed roof and a pleasing façade, with an old-fashioned garden. In the middle of the 18th century it was a country retreat well away from the town. It was here that the young writer and philosopher Rousseau lived for five years with the more mature Madame de Warens and her gardener, Claude Anet, a curious but apparently contented ménage-à-trois. Rousseau was settled enough to write several books there. The house now belongs to the municipality of Chambéry, and it was completely restored in 1978 exactly as Rousseau described it in his famous *Confessions*. The garden looks over

Alleyways like this are one of the appealing features of Chambéry

the valley of Chambéry and across to Mont Nivolet. The property is open to the public, morning and afternoon, all year round, except on Tuesdays and public holidays.

Not wishing to sound too much like an old-fashioned gramophone record with the needle stuck in a groove, I have tried to avoid going on too much about the magnificent scenery of Savoy. It is all sensational and you cannot escape it. From Chambéry it is an easy drive by a picturesque mountain road, the D916, which crosses the Col de l'Epine, and then the D921 to the **Lac d'Aiguebelette**. Though nothing like as large as the Lac du Bourget or the Lac d'Annecy, Aiguebelette is still sizeable, covering 550ha. The lake is very deep, completely unpolluted, and very good for fishing. As no motorised boats are allowed, it is tranquil. The western and southern shores have several equipped bathing beaches, and boats and pedalos can be hired. A pretty road circumnavigates the shore, a distance of 17km, with several good viewpoints. At La Combe there is a pleasant café-restaurant, which also has simple rooms to let.

Aix-les-Bains, 15km north of Chambéry, is built on a slight elevation above the eastern shore of the Lac du Bourget. Behind the town rise the limestone heights of Mont Revard, and in front it looks across the blue waters of the lake to the sharp ridge of the Cat's Tooth mountain (Dent du Chat) on the other side. Eighteen kilometres long and more than 3km wide, it is the largest mountain lake in France, and from its northern end it is linked to the river Rhône by the Canal de Savières. Water normally flows from the lake down the canal to the Rhône, but when the Rhône is in flood the flow is from the river to the lake.

Aix-les-Bains today is a clean and prosperous-looking place but it did not always give this impression to visitors. In 1773 Charles Burney, a friend of Dr Samuel Johnson and the father of Fanny Burney, the novelist and diarist, wrote

> We visited the famous hot baths here ... built by the Emperor Gratian. There are several Roman inscriptions and many other antiquities, but nothing can have a more antique and ruinous

The prosperous lakeside spa of Aix-les-Bains has a picturesque marina

appearance than the whole town which, however, is in summer a good deal frequented on account of its waters, in despite of every inconvenience of bad lodging, provisions, etc.

Things have changed. Aix-les-Bains is now said to have 95 hotels, eight of them first class. But Burney was writing six years before the building of the first 'modern' thermal establishment in 1779, and it was not until the 1860s, when Napoleon III made spas fashionable that Aix really began to expand. Its new National Thermal Establishment was built in 1864 and enlarged in 1881. Another building, the Nouvelles Thermes, was erected in 1934 and enlarged and modernised in 1972.

The national spa specialises in the treatment of rheumatism and allied conditions, and in another part of Aix the Marlioz Thermal Establishment treats respiratory ailments.

The National Thermal Establishment is open to visitors, who are shown the modern installations and then the earlier buildings with some Roman remains, including a hot bath and a circular swimming pool.

Other Roman remains in the town are the Arc de Campanus, and the Temple of Diana, both in the same locality opposite the Nouvelles Thermes. The Temple of Diana now houses a small museum of archaeology.

Lovers of fine arts should not miss the Musée Faure which contains a fine collection of pictures and sculpture and is particularly strong in Impressionist works. Degas, Vuillard, Pisarro, Sisley, and Cézanne are among the artists represented, and there is a series of superb bronzes by Rodin, as well as works by other famous sculptors,

including Carpeaux and Maillol. Those who prefer pictures on playing cards will be glad to know that there is an excellent casino in Aix.

Boat trips on the Lac du Bourget vary from one hour to all afternoon, and there is a four-hour trip which takes you out of the lake and down the 3km Canal de Savières to the Rhône and back. One of the best excursions is to the **Abbaye de Haute-combe**, because it not only takes you diagonally across the lake, offering mountain views in all directions, but also allows you ashore to see something of the abbey. On Sundays and some holidays there is an 8.30 boat service to the abbey to hear 9.15 mass, with Gregorian chant.

Hautecombe, originally a 12th-century Cistercian foundation, is now a Benedictine abbey. Its cemetery is the burial place of more than 40 princes and princesses of the House of Savoy, including Umberto II, the last king of Italy, who was buried there in March 1983.

The abbey buildings are attractive but not old, and the only parts open to the public are the church and the 12th-century Grange Batelière, a kind of combined boathouse and barn. This building, which has an undercover dock with a ramp up which boats could be pulled, and a floor above which was used for storing the monks' agricultural produce, is unique in France. The upper floor now has an exhibition of the life and work of Benedictine monks. The church was restored in the 19th century in what can best be described as rather exuberant Italian Gothic style. The interior contains marble, stone and gilded wooden statues in profusion, that is to say some hundreds.

The Abbey of Hautecombe, standing beside Lac du Bourget

About 10km north of Aix there is a hamlet called **La Chambotte** where there is a belvedere with a panoramic view of the Lac du Bourget. Take the *route nationale* N201 (not the *autoroute*) towards Annecy for about 5km. At La Biolle turn left on to the D991B, go through the village of Villette, about 4km, keeping left, and then turn left at St Germain, and start climbing. Though the Michelin Red Guide recommends this viewpoint it does not mention that the view is completely blocked by a bar-restaurant and that, as the Michelin Green Guide does explain, the view is from the terrace at the back of the restaurant. By chance it was late in the season when I was there and the place was closed, but I was able to reach the terrace by climbing a gate. There can be few better places to enjoy a cool drink on a fine summer afternoon. Pity it was closed.

Hotels & Restaurants

Prices: A = Very Expensive, B = Expensive, C = Moderately Expensive, D = Average, E = Cheap.

AIX-LES-BAINS (73100 Savoie): **Le Manoir,** 37 rue Georges-ler (79 61 44 00). Nicely situated in the upper town behind the spa. Comfortable. Good restaurant. Rooms C. Meals B.
Davat, le Grand Port (79 35 09 63). A good Logis de France close to the lakeside and the marina. M. Davat is a first-class chef and an amiable host. Rooms D. Meals C–D.
Pastorale, 221 av du Grand Port (79 35 25 36). Roomy, modernised interior, family run. Rooms C. Meals D.
Hôtel de la Cloche, 9 bld Wilson (79 35 01 06). Spacious, well run, comfortable. Rooms B–C. Meals C–D.
Lille, le Grand Port (79 35 04 22). Fine terrace overlooking the lake. First-class but somewhat overpriced. Meals B.
Brasserie Poste, 32 av Victoria (79 35 00 65). Meals D–E.

ALBERTVILLE (73200 Savoie): **Million,** 8 pl Liberté (79 32 25 15). Good hotel with a first-class restaurant. Million is the name of the chef-proprietor, not what it costs to eat there! Rooms C–D. Meals B–C, but good value.
Le Roma, route de Chambéry (79 37 15 56). One km outside the town on the main road; excellent value. Rooms and meals D.

ANNECY (74000 Haute Savoie) **AND LAC D'ANNECY: L'Abbaye,** 15 chemin Abbaye, Annecy-le-Vieux (50 23 61 08). Spacious, comfortable, good service. Only 8 rooms. Good restaurant. Rooms B.
Au Faisan Doré, 34 av d'Albigny (50 23 02 46). 40 rooms. Nicely situated near the lake. Modern, comfortable interior. Good value restaurant. Logis de France. Rooms C. Meals D.
Ibis, 12 rue de la Gare (50 45 43 21). One of the well-known chain, pleasantly situated in the old town. Rooms D. Meals D–E.
Auberge de L'Eridan, 7 av de Chavoires, Annecy-le-Vieux (50 66 22 04). Direct and unpretentious, M. Marc Veyrat is one of the great chefs of France, and his restaurant is probably the best in the region, though they won't agree with that in Talloires. Meals A.
Didier Roque, 13 rue Jean Mermoz, Annecy-le-Vieux (50 23 07 90). Serious *haute cuisine* from the chef proprietor. Quite expensive but good value menus. Meals C–E.
Le Matafan, quais de l'Evêche (50 45 53 87). Beside the canal in the picturesque old town. Excellent value. Meals D–E.
Le Pichet, 13 rue Perrière (50 45 32 41). Also in *la vieille ville.* Sound and unpretentious. Meals D–E.
Auberge du Père Bise, route du Port, **Talloires,** 74290 Veyrier-du-Lac (50 60 72 01).

A hotel for the rich, with a restaurant well known throughout France. Romantically situated beside the lake, luxurious, the hotel cannot be faulted (Relais et Châteaux). Superb though it is, the restaurant is now perhaps rather overpriced. Rooms A+. Meals A+.

L'Abbaye de Talloires, route du Port, **Talloires**, 74290 Veyrier-du-Lac (50 60 77 33). A 17th-century former Benedictine Abbey beautifully converted to a luxury hotel (Relais et Châteaux), with rooms around the cloisters. Lakeside terrace. Rooms A+. Meals A.

Beau Site, Talloires, 74290 Veyrier-du-Lac (50 60 71 04). Pleasant hotel in five-acre grounds with private beach on the lake. Rooms and meals C–D.

Villa des Fleurs, Talloires, 74290 Veyrier-du-Lac (50 60 71 14). Small Logis de France (7 rooms) with a very good restaurant. Rooms D. Meals C–D.

Hôtel le Roselet, 74410 St Jorioz (50 68 67 19). On the lakeside in the pretty village of **Duingt**, but also close to the main road. Sound Logis de France. Rooms and meals D.

Hôtel La Chataigneraie, 74210 Faverges (50 44 30 67). Family-run Logis de France in pleasant situation at Chaparon, near lake. Rooms and meals D.

Note: Check before booking — in many hotels around Lake Annecy half-board is obligatory in the high season.

CHAMBÉRY (73000 Savoie): **Les Princes**, 4 rue de Boigne (near the Elephant Foundation) (79 33 45 36). Attractive, comfortable rooms, and first-class restaurant. Rooms D. Meals C–D.

Novotel, à la Motte Servolex, 73000 Chambéry (79 69 21 27). In the country 3km outside town. One of the world-wide chain, modern, reliable. Restaurant sound but nothing special. Rooms C–D. Meals C.

CHAMONIX (74400 Haute Savoie): **L'Arveyron**, chemin des Cristalliers (50 53 18 29). Good value modest hotel. Rooms and meals D–E.

Les Gentianes, Le Lavancher (50 54 01 31). Comfortable family hotel of traditional mountain chalet style. Rooms D–E. Meals D.

EVIAN-LES-BAINS (74500 Haute Savoie): **La Verniaz**, route d'Abondance, Neuvecelle (50 75 04 90). Rooms in chalets overlooking Lake Geneva, very comfortable. Amenities include heated pool and tennis. Good restaurant. Rooms and meals A–B.

Le Moulin à Poivre, Neuvecelle (50 75 21 84). A Logis de France with better than average restaurant. Rooms and meals D–E.

Chez Tante Marie, Bernex (50 73 60 35). Between the village of Bernex and the countryside. Flowers everywhere. Another family-run Logis de France, where the proprietor is the chef, and a good one. Rooms D. Meals D–E.

Museums, Châteaux etc; opening times

Note: am/pm means closed for lunch (normally for two hours); cable cars etc in winter resorts also operate in summer, but operating and opening times vary from place to place, so it is best to enquire at the local tourist information office.

CHAMBÉRY: Museum of Fine Arts, all year round, am/pm. Closed Tue and public holidays.

CHAMONIX: Alpine Museum, afternoons from Christmas to Easter and June–Sept. **Les Charmettes**, all year round, am/pm. Closed Tue and public holidays.

THONON-LES-BAINS: Château de Ripaille (between Evian and Thonon), daily am/pm from 1 June to 30 Sept. Mid-April to end May, and October, Mon–Fri pm only, Sat, Sun and holidays am/pm.

Leisure

AIX-LES-BAINS, boat excursions, boat hire on Lac du Bourget, rock climbing, horse riding, mountain walking, 18-hole golf course.

ANNECY AND LAC D'ANNECY, dinner cruises on the lake, boat hire, 18-hole golf course.

Tourist Information Offices

AIX-LES-BAINS – pl M. Mollard (79 35 05 92)

ANNECY – clos Bonlieu, 1 rue Jean Jaurès (50 45 00 33)

CHAMONIX – pl Triangle de l'Amitié (50 53 00 24)

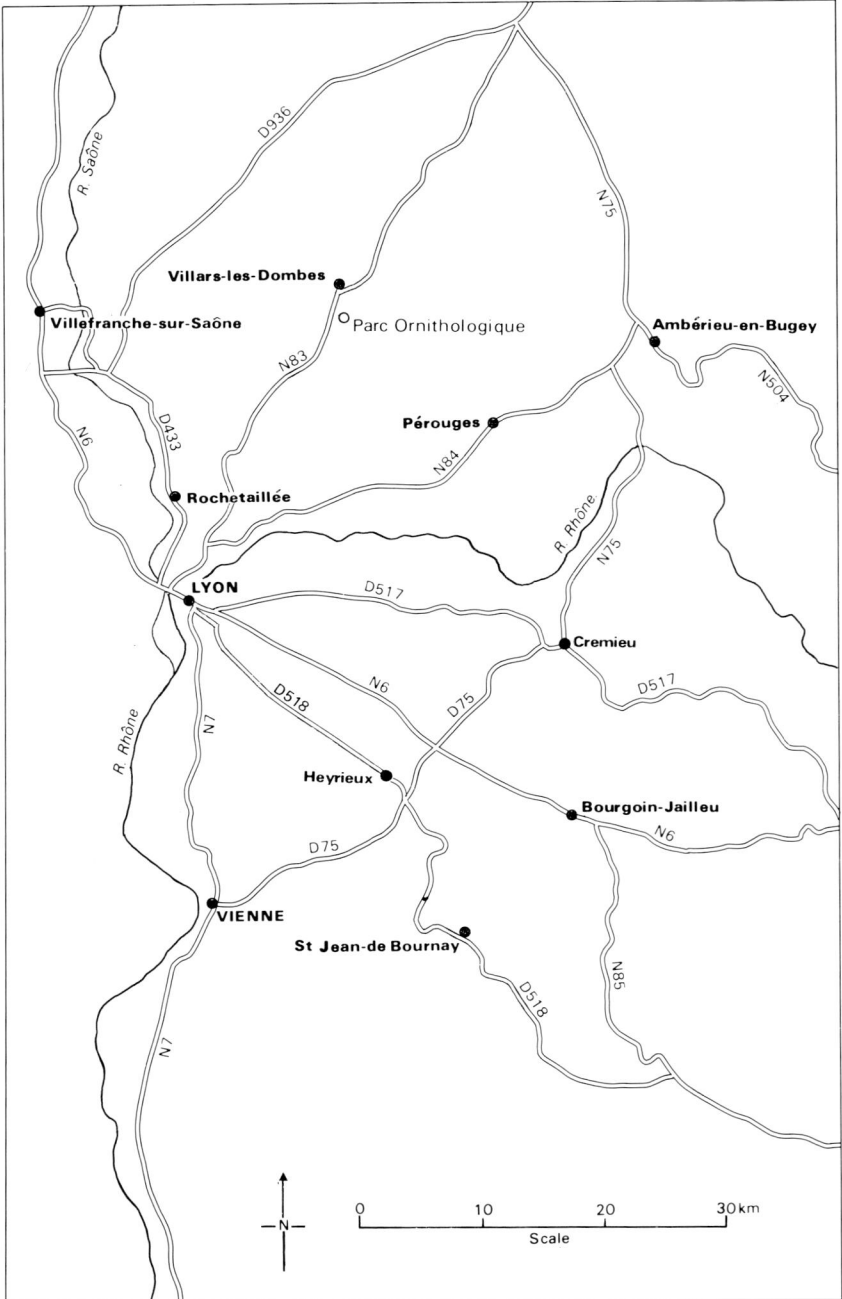

5
Lyon and the Lyonnais

Any resemblance between the characteristics of Lyon and any other city, living or dead, is purely coincidental. This is, of course, an exaggeration but it suffices to indicate that the second city of France really is an exceptional place. Two things lie at the root of Lyon's individuality: first its great age — it is already more than 50 years since Lyon celebrated its 2,000th anniversary; and secondly its very attractive situation. It grew up around the confluence of two great rivers of entirely different character, the tempestuous Rhône and the placid Saône, and on the two sizeable and picturesque hills which look down on the two rivers.

Lyon (pop. 1,200,000) is about the same size as Birmingham, and like Birmingham it is a commercial and heavily industrialised city; that is all they have in common. This, too, is an exaggeration. Lyon, like all industrial towns has its defeated suburbs and its interminable grey and gloomy streets, and it is known for the river mists that sometimes fill the valley and pervade the city, adding a cloak of secrecy to the already self-contained nature of its people. But it is the differences not the similarities which give towns their

character, and in addition to its fine situation, Lyon has some of the best Renaissance streets in Europe, medieval houses, lovely old squares, historic buildings and unsurpassed shops and restaurants, and it is packed with the evidence of man's genius in arts and science, and of 2,000 years of social development.

Although there was an earlier Gallic settlement, Lyon, like most towns of any consequence in France, was founded by the Romans, and in this case it was an official foundation. Some Roman colonists had been settled in the older town of Vienne, but the local tribe took umbrage and drove them out. In 43BC a Roman general, Plancus, was ordered by the Senate to resettle these refugees at the site which is now Lyon.

The new city was called Lugdunum, and once he had carried out his orders and marked out its limits on the hill of Fourvières, Plancus appears to have lost all interest in it. This was not true of the new Caesar, Augustus, and his son-in-law Agrippa. With the usual Roman efficiency they put in hand the work of making the city an important crossroads and metropolis. Five great Roman roads were built, towards

Aquitaine, towards the north, towards the Mediterranean, towards Italy and Switzerland, and towards the Rhine. Four great aqueducts brought water to the new town. Under the influence of sound planning and good communications it developed rapidly. In 10AD its importance was emphasised when representatives of the 60 tribes of Gaul gathered there for the inauguration of a temple symbolising the deification of Augustus.

Another Roman emperor associated with Lyon was Claudius, who was born there on that same day in 10AD, and who eventually gave his birthplace colonial status, so that its inhabitants became Roman citizens. The Emperor Caligula lived in Lyon for part of his short rule, and was just as mad there as he was in Rome. The first thing he did on arrival was to have a list drawn up of all the richest citizens, kill them, and confiscate their goods. His love of money was such that he even banished his sisters and sold their furniture. From time to time he would stand outside his palace begging for money.

In its early days Lyon had the unfortunate gift of backing the wrong horse. Its citizens supported Nero in his struggle against Galba. Naturally, when Galba won he did nothing for Lyon. Later, they were wrong again when they backed Albin against Septimus Severus. So as the Roman Empire in the west declined, so did the fortunes of Lyon. When Roman authority failed altogether, the city was several times taken by Barbarian invaders from Germany. One of these tribes, the Burgondes, from whom Burgundy took its name, settled in Lyon and made it their capital, but in 500AD they were defeated by another

Germanic tribe, the Franks, under the leadership of Clovis. This chief was the founder of the first royal house of France, the Merovingians.

Very little is known of the history of Lyon in the Dark Ages which followed. In 580AD there was a terrible flood in which the whole of the lower town was drowned and only the fleetest of foot escaped to take refuge on the hills. It is also known that in 732AD Lyon was captured by the Moors, who had invaded France after conquering most of Spain. Thousands of its inhabitants were slaughtered, and religious buildings and the city's fortifications were destroyed. The town was liberated a few years later by Charles Martel who defeated the Moors at a spot near the Dordogne, where today a village commemorates his name. Even in this the Lyonnais were unlucky, because Martel's troops made off with everything of value which the Moors had overlooked.

The most important aspect of life in Lyon in the early Middle Ages was the dominance of the Church. Its hold on the city was so tight and its taxes so heavy that the citizens several times rebelled. In 1307 Lyon was formally united with the crown of France, and in 1320 Philip the Good, King of France, signed a treaty with the Archbishop of Savoy which put an end to the absolute power of the Church in Lyon, and its administration was taken over by a town council.

But the city's troubles were not over. It had hardly settled to the new regime when, like the rest of Europe, it was devastated in 1348 by the Black Death. So many people died that commercial activity was reduced to almost nothing, and it took the city the best part of 100 years to recover its position. It was not until 1419, when the Lyon Fairs were instituted by royal decree, that the town really began to develop. The Fairs were established with the object of attracting foreign merchants, and they were given incentives to persuade them to settle there and build up trade connections. There was no taxation and the currencies of all countries were allowed to circulate freely at their proper exchange value. Bills of exchange could be given, and traders could carry on business on the same basis as in their own countries. Every year there were four periods of 15 days each when the Fairs were allowed to take place under these favourable conditions. Considerable benefits resulted in a relatively short time, and the city soon became a centre of international trade and international banking. In 1466 there were already 15 Florentine banks established there, and within 40 years the number had grown to 46. The Florentines were not the only ones. Bankers also came from Milan, Genoa, and even Flanders, Switzerland and Germany. The first letter of credit was issued in Lyon.

The period of expansion that began with the Fairs continued unbroken until the French Revolution.

Even in the 1st century AD there had been a textile industry in Lyon with associations of workers specialising in making clothes in wool, linen, canvas, and skins. But it was silk for which Lyon was eventually to become famous. In 1536 Francis I allowed Genoese silk workers to settle in Lyon, permitted all silk workers to use their own premises, and exempted them from all taxation. By 1626 there were 1,479 silk masters and apprentices,

and by 1660 the number had grown to 3,310.

It was not only goods and wealth which flowed into and out of Lyon in the 16th and 17th centuries. It was a natural crossroads of Europe and thinkers and philosophers of all countries passed through it and disseminated their ideas. Some stayed. It was therefore natural that, parallel with the development of banking and the silk industry, Lyon became a centre of printing. The first book sent out from the presses of Lyon was produced by Guillaume le Roy, a printer of Flemish origin, in 1473, nearly 20 years before Columbus discovered America.

Another famous printer, Sebastien Gryphis, whose books are today collectors' items, came from Germany and was naturalised in Lyon in 1523. There were so many printers in the city during the 16th century that they established their own quarter in the rue Mercière and adjoining streets.

The growth of printing brought a revival of the study of the classics of Greece and Rome. Instead of the physical sciences and theology, men now sought scholarship in literature, philosophy and art. Printing presses liberated human thought, removing it from the control of the Church and the ruling princes. In the 13th century the Albigensian heresy had been bloodily destroyed by the sword, but in the 16th century it proved to be impossible to crush the more extreme Lutheran heresy, despite even bloodier wars and the united efforts of the King of France, the popes and the Inquisition. The new ideas were spread by books and pamphlets to thousands where in the past they could be spread only by word of mouth to a few people at a time. So the Renaissance

A scene in the medieval pl de la Basoche, old Lyon

and the Reformation followed directly from the invention and rapid spread of printing, and Lyon was at the heart of these movements in France.

The religious wars of the 16th century left their mark on Lyon. The city was captured and held by Protestant troops for more than a year. The Catholic churches were sacked, and the cloisters· of the cathedral of St Jean were destroyed, statues smashed, and the bells melted down.

When, in 1572 the notorious massacre of Protestants took place on the eve of St Bartholomew in Paris, the Catholics of Lyon followed suit. Protestants in prison were massacred, and others, roped together by the neck, were thrown into the Rhône.

Many of the silk weavers and printers had left Lyon during the religious wars, but at the end of the 16th century King Henri IV reestablished the Lyon Fairs, with all their advantages, and this soon led to a revival of the silk industry and the economy.

Despite the swingeing taxation imposed on Lyon by the monarchy's successive ministers, Richelieu, Mazarin and Colbert, Lyon continued to increase in prosperity and vitality. It set up its own Academy of Science and Literature. The first veterinary school in Europe was founded in Lyon by a M. Claude Bourgelat in 1762. A family of botanists from Lyon, the brothers, Antoine, Bernard, and Joseph de Jussieu greatly influenced the study of plant life. In 1783 the Montgolfier brothers had demonstrated balloon flight in the nearby town of Annonay. The following year they were invited to Lyon by the Academy, and made a successful flight with themselves and five other passengers in the basket. In the same year the Marquis Jouffroy d'Abbans, who had invented a steam engine to power boats, made a trip of a few hundred metres against the current on the Saône at Lyon. So towards the end of the 18th century Lyon was a city where industry, art and science all flourished.

But it all came down with a crash during the French Revolution. At first the inhabitants welcomed it, but it was soon evident that the population was divided between hard-core revolutionaries and moderates who, though attached to the idea of liberty, were also loyal to the monarchy. When King Louis XVI was executed in January 1793 there was open conflict between the two parties in Lyon, and in July the population rebelled against the Revolution and sent its chief officer in Lyon, Marie-Joseph Chalier, to the guillotine. As a result, the order was given in Paris for Lyon to be destroyed.

On 7 August 1793, troops of the Revolutionary Government arrived at the gates of Lyon and demanded the city's surrender. With 40,000 men under arms, the city refused and heavy losses were inflicted on the government troops in the attacks which followed. Lyon was besieged for two months before being obliged to surrender.

The victorious general, Dubois-Crancé, took literally the decree that Lyon was to be destroyed. His second in command, Couthon, struck the first hammer blow in the destruction of the houses in the place Bellecour, in the heart of Lyon.

A list of 20,000 suspects was drawn up. and executions by groups were started. When the guillotine proved too slow a method of dealing with the condemned, they were taken in groups of a hundred or more to wasteland on the outskirts of the city, where they were slaughtered by cannon fire and grapeshot.

Robespierre, who had been the effective leader of France for a year, was himself guillotined because of his extremism. His death brought the Terror to an end, and Lyon was spared further carnage and destruction.

When Napoleon returned to France from Italy and Egypt in 1799, he was enthusiastically welcomed by the inhabitants as he passed through Lyon. When he became First Consul in 1800, he remembered Lyon and came himself to lay the first stone in the rebuilding of the place Bellecour, destroyed by Couthon. Under Napoleon, Lyon rose again from its ruins and entered on a new period of economic growth. As Emperor he encouraged things by ordering two new bridges to be built across the Saône, and by founding the Museum and the School of Fine Arts. Always indulgent towards his family, and aware of the value of powerful family connections, he made his uncle, Cardinal Fesch, Archbishop of Lyon.

In 1804 M. Jacquard, the son of a silk worker, perfected a loom which enabled one weaver to produce as much as five workers could do on the old looms. Afraid of the loss of employment, weavers destroyed the first examples of Jacquard's loom. But Napoleon realised the importance of the invention and paid Jacquard a bonus of 50 francs for every loom put into use, and later gave him a pension. The new looms required higher ceilings than those in the Renaissance buildings where most of the weavers worked. The silk masters put up streets of tall, narrow houses on the hill of La Croix Rousse for the new looms, and for the weavers to live and work. These jerry-built houses had no comfort whatever, and the wretched conditions together with poor rates of pay led to armed workers' revolts in 1831 and 1834. They gained minimal concessions.

In 1875 another key development in the silk industry took place when a mechanical loom was introduced. Soon only a few handlooms were left, used for the weaving of luxury fabrics.

Lyon today is still one of the world's most important centres for the manufacture of silk, and also has a high production of synthetic fibres.

Apart from textiles there are other large industries in Lyon. Almost 100,000 workers are employed in various branches of the metal industry — foundries, mechanical engineering,

LYON CITY CENTRE

wire manufacture. A third of all the electric motors produced in France are made in Lyon.

There is also an important chemical industry concentrating on dyes, pharmaceutical and photographic products. Its old speciality of banking and insurance is still of international importance in the city. Lyon is also one of Europe's chief centres of scientific and medical research. In 542AD, Ultrogoth, the daughter-in-law of Clovis, founded a hospice in Lyon for the sick and needy. Called the Hôtel-Dieu, it is today one of Europe's greatest hospitals, known throughout the medical world for its advanced techniques.

During the Second World War Lyon was at the heart of the Resistance movement. A number of different groups and underground newspapers grew up independently. In 1941, the former prefect of the Eure et Loire department, Jean Moulin, who was to become one of the great heroes of the Resistance, arrived in the city. He spent two years uniting the different Resistance movements and coordinating their activities. In June 1943 he was betrayed and arrested by the Gestapo. He was tortured for several days and died while being transported to Germany. The activities of the Maquis continued and many Resistance members were killed in attacks on German installations, and in Lyon itself. In 1944 the Germans destroyed almost every suspension bridge on the Rhône.

Lyon is today a prosperous city, and its bourgeois citizens have the reputation throughout France of being difficult to know. It is said that they make discretion a cardinal virtue and dislike all forms of show or boasting. The Lyonnais themselves claim to be straightforward people who enjoy family life and the company of old friends. They like to stroll along the riverside, or through the old quarters, or in the lovely Parc de la Tête d'Or, where a million roses bloom every June. They say they invented boules and they play and watch it a great deal. They like to pass the time with friends over a glass of Beaujolais in one of the cafés, and above all they enjoy the superb Lyonnais cuisine in their personal favourite among the scores of first-class restaurants.

Lyon was the first town in France to benefit from la loi Malraux which, in the early sixties, provided for the preservation and restoration of historic old quarters. With its hundreds of Renaissance and medieval buildings, its Romanesque and Gothic churches, its 24 museums, there is so much to see in Lyon that a choice has to be made. What follows is a personal selection.

The heart of Lyon is the Presqu'île, the peninsula between the Rhône and the Saône north of their confluence. The heart of the Presqu'île is the place Bellecour, and this is the best place to begin. This famous, leafy square, 6ha in area, is one of the largest in Europe. (The underground car park is huge, so remember where you put your car.) The buildings destroyed during the Revolution, on the east and west sides, were replaced by symmetrical buildings in the Louis XVI style, and it was Napoleon himself who laid the first stone in 1800. The gardens which formerly occupied much of the square were removed during the works for the underground car park, and have not yet been replaced, though there are fountains, flower beds and a flower market in

Place Bellecour in the heart of the old city, Lyon

one corner. The equestrian statue in the middle is of Louis XIV, and was erected in 1825 to replace an earlier one melted down during the revolution. The clock tower which can be seen at the Rhône end of the square, is all that remains of the Hospice de la Charite, which was for 300 years the most important hospital in Lyon after the Hôtel-Dieu. It was founded with surplus money collected to help the poor and needy in times of hardship. It was thus the first example of public assistance or social service.

From the north-west corner of the place Bellecour it is an easy walk across the pont Bonaparte to the St Jean quarter, the most interesting part of the old town. The narrow streets here are lined with the finest collection of late medieval and Renaissance buildings to be found anywhere in France. They vary from comfortable houses to the mansions and palaces of rich merchants and bankers. On every side there are pointed towers and turrets, mullioned windows, coats of arms carved in stone over arched doorways, spiral staircases characteristic of these houses towards the end of the 16th century, and decorative Italianate carving used on the exterior of the later Renaissance houses. A vaulted passage leads under the first floor of many of the houses to an interior courtyard open to the sky. There was normally a well in a corner of the courtyard, and many of these remain.

A renaissance courtyard in Lyon old town

There were open galleries around the courtyard but in some cases these have been closed to give more living space.

It is pleasant to wander round and absorb the atmosphere, even if you do not know what you are looking at, but it is more rewarding to take a guided tour (there is a Tourist Office in the square opposite St Jean Cathedral). As a compromise between the two, you could walk down the rue St Jean to the place du Change and on through the St Paul quarter via the rue Lainerie, in which numbers 10, 14 and 18 are fine examples of their period, and back through the rue Juiverie to the place du Change. In the rue Juiverie there are several fine mansions. At No. 4, the Paterine mansion is a typical example of the Renaissance style of

the great days of Lyon. At No. 8 the Bullioud mansion is another fine 16th-century construction. Its courtyard has galleries built on squinches, an idea brought from Italy in 1536 and used here for the first time in France. What is a squinch, you may ask. It is an arch linking the inside corner of walls at right angles, so that a gallery or tower may be built on it to join two wings of a building. The characteristic styles of old Lyon are also represented in the rue Juiverie at Nos. 10, 13, 23, and 20.

Once back in the place du Change, take the rue Soufflot and then turn into the rue Gadagne. Here you will

Overleaf: *Cafés such as this one in rue St Jean provide a good stopping-point as you explore Lyon*

find the most impressive example of the architecture of old Lyon, the Hôtel Gadagne. (*Hôtel* originally meant a town mansion, and is still used in that sense in France.) It was started in the 14th century and extended from time to time until the 16th. It was bought in 1445 by bankers of Italian origin, the Gadagne brothers, who were so wealthy that 'rich as Gadagne' became a saying in Lyon.

The mansion today houses the city's Historical Museum, and on the first floor there is a museum of puppets from all over the world.

Carry on from the rue Gadagne into the rue du Boeuf. On the corner of the place Neuve St Jean and the rue du Boeuf there is a small sculpture of an ox. This is a survivor of a system for indicating the name of a street for the many people who could not read. The Maison du Crible in the rue du Boeuf is famous for its tower and rose-coloured roughcast, from which the restaurant on the corner, La Tour Rose, one of the finest and most expensive in Lyon, takes its name.

The old quarters of Lyon have a very unusual feature which adds interest and a touch of mystery. Many of those vaulted passages leading from the street to an interior court-yard carry on from the other side under other buildings and out into another street. These covered passages, originally built to save space, are called *traboules*. These passages are still in everyday use, and the verb *trabouler* means to take short cuts through the old quarter using them. There are also many of them in the silk weavers' quarter on the hill of La Croix Rousse, where they were useful for carrying about the bolts of silk, protected from the weather.

One of the many traboules – *covered passages – leading from one street to another in Lyon*

Do not leave the old quarter without having a good look at the cathedral of St Jean. The building, started in 1180 but not finished until 300 years later, combines several successive architectural styles. The transept and the apse are Romanesque, the nave and the towers are early Gothic, and the façade and some of the chapels are late Gothic. The interior is lit by fine stained-glass windows. Those in the lower part of the choir date from the 13th century, others are almost as old but have been considerably restored. Near the choir there is a vast astronomical clock made in the 14th century. At midday, one o'clock, two o'clock and three o'clock, it launches into an extraordinary performance in which bells ring, cocks crow, little doors open and puppet figures pop out and parade in various activities said to represent the Annunciation. The Astronomer Royal and the man who prepares the astronomical tables in Whitaker's Almanac may understand it but I doubt if anyone else does. It certainly bewildered Charles Dickens when he visited Lyon in the 1840s, and the clock was set in motion for him. He wrote:

Meanwhile the Sacristan stood, explaining these wonders, and pointing them out, severally, with a wand. There was a centre puppet of the Virgin Mary; and close to her, a small pigeon-hole, out of which another and very ill-looking puppet made one of the most sudden plunges I ever saw accomplished; instantly flopping back again at sight of her, and banging his little door violently after him. Taking this to be emblematic of the victory over Sin and Death, and not at all unwilling to show that I understood the subject, in anticipation of the showman, I rashly said, 'Aha! The Evil Spirit. To be sure. He is very soon disposed of.' 'Pardon, Monsieur,' said the Sacristan, with a polite motion of his hand towards the little door, as if introducing somebody — 'The Angel Gabriel!'

Take the funicular from near the cathedral to the top of the hill of Fourvière to see the extraordinary basilica of Notre-Dame. From the outside this much-turreted and crenellated building is, to say the least, bizarre. The interior has to be seen to be believed. There is hardly a square inch of floor, roof and walls which has not been twiddled and twirled, gilded and encrusted, marbled and mosaiced, bepillared and bestatued in an hysterical riot of overdecoration. But it does have the attraction for visitors that they have probably never seen anything like it before.

From the terrace beside the basilica there is an extensive view over the city, dominated in the middle distance by the skyscraper of the Credit Lyonnais, known to the locals as 'the pencil' because it comes to a point. If you come down the steps from the basilica and turn left, a short walk brings you to the Gallo-Roman Museum.

This museum is an absolute must for anyone with the slightest interest in classical times, and a triumph of modern architecture, cleverly set in the hillside itself, with great picture windows overlooking the Roman theatre. The five floors of exhibits include some wonderful mosaics, statuary, and the unique Claudian bronze tablet, discovered in La Croix Rousse in 1538, beautifully engraved with the speech which the Emperor Claudius made to the Senate in 48AD requesting Roman citizenship for the inhabitants of Lyon.

The fine Roman theatre next to the museum is about the same size as those in Arles and Orange, and is the oldest in France. Originally built in pre-Christian times it was enlarged early in the 2nd century, under the Emperor Hadrian, to take up to 10,000 spectators. The tiers of seats have been restored so that the theatre can

Overleaf: *A panoramic view of the city can be enjoyed from Lyon cathedral, Notre-Dame de Fourvière*

be used for modern performances. A paved Roman road leads around the top, and adjacent to the big theatre there is an exactly similar theatre on a smaller scale, the odeon. These smaller theatres, from which so many modern cinemas took their name, were used for conferences and concerts. The orchestra platform has been rebuilt in rose, grey, and green stone, in the original attractive geometric pattern.

The funicular near the Roman theatre is not the one you came up by, but leads directly back to the same departure point near the cathedral of St Jean.

From the north-east corner of the place Bellecour the rue du Président Herriot leads to another famous square of old Lyon, the place des Terreaux, a walk of slightly less than 1km. Apart from its lively café terraces, this square has two important buildings, and a rather nice public fountain by Bartholdi, the sculptor of the Statue of Liberty. The whole of the east side of the place des Terreaux is occupied by the imposing façade of the Hôtel de Ville. Although Lyon was being taxed to the limit by the king's ministers in the middle of the 17th century, the town councillors showed an uncharacteristic lack of prudence throughout this period. They spent heavily on receptions and ceremonies of all kinds and, on top of that decided to build themselves a magnificent new Town Hall. It was started in 1646 but, as money was in short supply, it was not finished until 1672. Two years later most of the façade was destroyed in a serious fire. There was no money to restore it, and in 1677 the city went bankrupt. It was more than 20 years before they were able to start the restoration, and then they called in

Jules-Hardouin Mansart, architect of Les Invalides and the place Vendôme in Paris and the Grand Trianon at Versailles. He rebuilt the façade in a completely different style, adding another floor, so that what you see today is an 18th-century façade on a 17th-century building.

The splendid monumental fountain in the centre of the place des Terreaux, with its four prancing horses, meant to symbolise the great rivers of France dashing to the ocean, is the work of Bartholdi, the 19th-century sculptor who was also responsible for the statue of the Gallic hero, Vercingetorix, in Clermont Ferrand, and the Statue of Liberty.

The whole of the south side of the place des Terreaux is taken up by the Palais St Pierre, a former Benedictine convent for the daughters of the nobility. The building, reconstructed at the end of the 17th century is rather severe but there is a charming courtyard garden where the old cloisters used to be. The building now houses the city's first-class Museum of Fine Arts. Apart from a collection of Egyptian, Roman, Byzantine, and Etruscan *objets d'art*, there is a superb collection of paintings of all periods. Old masters are represented by Veronese, Tintoretto, Rubens, El Greco, Cranach the Elder, Zurbaran, and artists of the Flemish and Dutch schools. There is a completely representative collection of the French schools of the 17th, 18th, 19th, and 20th centuries, right up to contemporary painters such as Hartung and de Stael. There are flower paintings from all periods which were used as sources of inspiration by the designers of silk fabrics over the years.

Lyon has 24 museums and no tourist will want to see all of them,

A Tragedy: The Story of Cinq-Mars

An extraordinary story came to an end in the place des Terreaux on 12 September 1642. Antoine Coeffier-Ruze, Marquis d'Effiat, was a marshal of France, and also Superintendent of Finance for Richelieu, and his close friend. At the height of a brilliant political and military career he died suddenly at 51, leaving a wife, two daughters and three sons. The eldest daughter married an eccentric cousin of Richelieu. He was a short-tempered man who calmed his rages by eating candles. The second daughter, faced with this example, retired to a Dominican convent where she lived to a great age. The eldest son died raving mad at 32. The youngest son led such a debauched and scandalous life that he was eventually banished. The hopes of the family were centred on the second son.

This young man, the Marquis de Cinq-Mars, was both very handsome and highly intelligent. From the age of 13 he spent his life at court. Louis XIII, a strange, pious man of low-geared and dubious sexuality, was completely infatuated by this beautiful youth. He made him his lieutenant for the Bourbonnais at the age of 15. Richelieu made him Master of the Royal Wardrobe when he was 18. Only a year later Louis promoted him to Grand Equerry. If Cinq-Mars was absent from the Court he was expected to write Louis two letters a day.

All these favours turned the head of Cinq-Mars, who demanded more and more. But the honey turned to vinegar and the relationship between the king, the cardinal, and the young marquis ended in mutual hatred. Richelieu became jealous and tried to turn the king against Cinq-Mars. In retaliation Cinq-Mars launched a plot with the Duke de Bouillon and his friend, Gaston d'Orleans, the king's brother, with the object of bringing about Richelieu's downfall. The plot was discovered, and Gaston d'Orleans betrayed his associates.

On that September day the crowds packed into the place des Terreaux, eager to watch the execution of the beautiful but over-ambitious young Marquis. Cinq-Mars was just 22.

The news was brought to Louis in the royal kitchens where he was amusing himself by helping to make jam. He went on stirring for some moments in silence and then is said to have muttered, 'The soul of Cinq-Mars was as black as the bottom of this pot.'

but on the way back to the place Bellecour, there is one which is rather special, just off the rue du Président Herriot, the Museum of Printing and Banking. This museum illustrates Lyon's enormous contribution to the early days of printing, and has exhibitions showing the earliest woodcuts, the development of typography, paging and binding techniques. There are many early editions of great value. Other rooms show the growth of banking and commerce in the town which issued the first cheque and set up the first stock exchange.

But perhaps the most interesting of Lyon's many fine museums, because it is the most unusual, is the Historical

André Marie Ampère

André Marie Ampère was born in Lyon and spent his youth there. He was an electrical genius and became a teacher and then Professor of Physics at the famous Ecole Polytechnique in Paris. He was the original absent-minded professor, often a delight to his students, and sometimes an embarrassment to family and friends. His students gave up counting the number of times he cleaned the blackboard with his handkerchief and blew his nose on the duster. One day as he crossed the Pont des Arts on his way to the Polytechnique he stooped to pick up a stone and paused to examine it. Suddenly remembering his lecture he took out his watch to check the time. Realising he was late, he threw his watch in the Seine and put the pebble in his pocket.

Thinking about an algebraic problem one day, he took a piece of chalk out of his jacket and, to the amusement of passers-by, began to cover with equations the side of a bus which happened to be stationary in front of him. Another time, invited to dinner by friends, he forgot where he was and, thinking himself in his own house, announced in the middle of the meal, 'Really it is quite impossible to get this new cook to prepare a decent dinner.'

Despite his absent-mindedness Ampère was a great physicist who discovered among other things the relationship between electricity and magnetism. And whatever he may have forgotten, nobody concerned with electricity can possibly forget him. An ampère is a measure of the flow of electricity, and occurs, abbreviated to 'amp' on millions of electrical products every day all over the world.

Museum of Fabrics. This is situated about 300m south of the place Belle-cour, in the 18th-century Hôtel Villeroy in the rue de la Charité. This museum was founded more than 100 years ago by the Chamber of Commerce of Lyon. It contains a truly remarkable collection of rich fabrics and materials from the earliest Christian times up to the present day. There are Coptic tapestries more than 1,000 years old, and a fine collection of Byzantine and Persian fabrics. There is a splendid series of Persian and Turkish carpets from the 16th–18th centuries. Early European fabrics include rare Italian cloths from the 13th and 14th centuries, rich Renaissance velvets from Genoa, Florence, and Venice, and intricately embroidered materials of the 17th and 18th centuries. There are examples of French textiles of all kinds from the 17th century onwards, particularly the silks of Lyon. The wall hangings 'with pheasants and peacocks' made in Lyon for Catherine the Great of Russia in 1771 are on show, and there are two rooms devoted to designs of the 19th and 20th centuries.

Next door, another 18th-century mansion houses the Museum of Decorative Arts, which has fine 18th-century furniture by famous makers, as well as Gobelin, Aubusson, Beauvais and Flemish tapestries, and porcelain from St Cloud, Sèvres, and Meissen.

Anyone visiting Lyon in June should certainly make the short trip from the centre to the lovely Parc de la Tête d'Or, which is to the people of Lyon what Kew Gardens is to Londoners. The park, which gets its name from an old legend that a golden head of Christ was buried there, is to the north-east of the city and includes a zoo, a large aviary full of exotic birds, a botanical garden, an alpine garden and glasshouses with tropical and subtropical plants. There is a spacious lake bordered at one end by a rose garden said to carry a million blooms in midsummer.

There are some worthwhile short excursions to be made from Lyon. A visit to the Henri Malartre Vintage Car Museum makes a good family outing, and car enthusiasts will be enthralled. To reach it follow the D433 beside the Saône north from Lyon for 12km to Rochetaillée where the museum is signposted. In this 15th-century château and its grounds beside the river 200 vehicles are ex-hibited, and more than half of them date from before 1914. Other par-ticularly interesting vehicles include Hitler's 1942 armoured Mercedes, and the Hispano-Suiza coupé de ville used by General de Gaulle after the libera-tion of Paris. There are old motor-cycles, and racing bikes used by early winners of the Tour de France. Old Grand Prix racing cars are well repre-sented, among them a 1953 Ferrari.

Thirty-five kilometres north-east of Lyon via the N84 is the ancient village of **Pérouges**, one of the most pictur-esque in France. It was a village of weavers which found itself unable to compete with the mechanisation of the industry in the 19th century. Gradually the people abandoned it and from

1,500 the population had fallen by 1910 to 90 and many houses were falling into ruins. But just before it was too late a campaign to save the village was started and received the support of the Mayor of Lyon and the Ministry of Fine Arts. Over the years the village has steadily been restored, and has been given some life by artisans who have opened workshops and sell their products to tourists.

Pérouges is built on top of a small hill and has retained its fortifications. In 1468 it was attacked by the Dauphi-nois and was heavily damaged, so that a lot of it had to be rebuilt at that time, and this explains why so much of it is in good condition today. The best-preserved part of these fortifications is the Porte d'en Haut (the Upper Gate), and the village still has its narrow cobbled streets, often with a gutter down the middle. Many of the houses have beamed façades, mullioned windows and wide overhanging eaves. Most of the streets lead to the centre, the very picturesque market place (place de la Halle), where there is a splendid lime tree planted in 1792. From the place de la Halle all the streets radiate to the rue des Rhondes which encircles the village.

Pérouges, which gets its name from its foundation by Italians from Perugia in pre-Roman times, was until 1601 an outpost of Savoy, and one of its finest houses is the Maison des Princes de Savoie, in the angle of the rue du Prince. The village has such a con-vincing atmosphere of the past that it has often been used for the setting of historical films such as The Three Musketeers and Twenty Years After. The only false note is produced by the shops of the artisans, completely devoted to tourism. But then without

The attractive market place is the heart of Pérouges

tourism Pérouges, and countless other old villages all over Europe, would be in ruins.

Pérouges lies at the southern extremity of one of the most unusual stretches of countryside in the whole of France, the region known as Les Dombes. The soil is impermeable here; water just lies on the surface. As long ago as the 14th century the farmers decided to turn this to their advantage by creating artificial lakes and ponds, which they then stocked with fish and waterfowl. After five or six years of harvesting the fish, they would empty the pond, plough and sow the land, which had become more fertile, and start another pond somewhere else. At one time there were more than 2,000 of these artificial lakes in

the area, but so much stagnant water bred fevers and life expectancy in Les Dombes was drastically reduced. It was the monks who showed the farmers how to achieve a healthier balance between land and water, and there are now about 1,000 of these *étangs* in an area which reaches north as far as Bourg-en-Bresse. The farmers take about 1,200 tons of fish (carp, pike, and tench) from them every year.

In the middle of the area at Villars-les-Dombes there is an excellent ornithological park with more than 400 different species of birds, very strong on waterfowl, but with tropical birds, vultures, flamingos, emus, ostriches, and other exotic species as well.

The town of **Vienne** is a destination in its own right, and people come

A timbered farmhouse typical of the Lyonnais region

from all over France to see it. But anyone visiting Lyon should take advantage of the fact that Vienne is only 30km to the south, and make this very worthwhile excursion. After Marseilles, Vienne is the city with the longest history in all France. Today it has rather a split personality. It not only has some of the finest Roman remains in France, interesting early Christian churches, and the ancient and splendid cathedral of St Maurice, but also the grim left-overs of 19th-century industrialisation, grey and sad-looking workers' houses and decaying factory shells. In Roman times it was known as Vienne the beautiful; it is perhaps not that today, but it still easily merits 'Vienne the fascinating'.

It is not a large town but it calls for patience on the part of the motorist. Whatever you do, do not try to enter the town from the junction by the

bridge as you arrive from Lyon. You are likely to get lost. Instead, carry on for another 500m beside the Rhône until you come to another junction with a wide turning on the left, and the Office de Tourisme on the corner. Turn down here, the cours Brillier, and the centre of town and almost everything of interest is immediately on your left. There is a car park in the first turning on the right off the cours Brillier, and parking metres at several locations in the centre. In the high season it may be easier to park on the other side of the Rhône and walk back over the footbridge.

A rich and prosperous city in Roman times, Vienne gradually faded away as the centuries passed. By the middle of the 17th century the population was only a third of what it had been. In 1651 the bridge was carried away by the Rhône in flood, and it

65

was the middle of the 19th century before there was enough money to replace it.

The Roman temple of Augustus and Livia is, with the Maison Carre at Nîmes, which it much resembles, the best preserved in France. A reason for this may be that in early Christian times it was converted into a church and the spaces between the pillars were walled in, and it was not until the 19th century that the temple was returned to its original form.

Not far from this temple is the Roman portico which marked the entrance to the forum, and nearby there are also vestigial remains of the temple and theatre of the goddess Cybele, 'mother of the gods', whose worship involved orgiastic rites. The Roman theatre, reached via the rue Pipet and the rue du Cirque, was completely buried under thousands of tons of earth until 1922, and it took six years of work to uncover it. Its 46 tiers could hold more than 13,000 spectators, making it one of the largest in Roman Gaul, bigger than those in Orange and Lyon. As at Lyon, it was accompanied by a smaller theatre, an odeon, which is not open to the public. In summer, performances are given in the Roman theatre.

If you continue up the rue Pipet to the top of the hill, there is an esplanade which offers a splendid view over the town and the cathedral of St Maurice and across the Rhône. The walk there and back takes about half an hour.

The very old Romanesque church of St André-le-Bas was renovated and the nave rebuilt in 1152 by Guillaume Martin, who signed and dated his work at the base of the second column on the right. There is a small but charming cloister of about the same date next to the church, and a terrace with a view across the Rhône to St Colombe and St Romain-en-Gal, which in Roman times were affluent suburbs of Vienne, and which are now interesting archaeological sites. Immediately to the north of St André-le-Bas is the Museum of Fine Arts with good Gallo-Roman antiquities, bronzes, ivories, jewellery, and some fine old ceramics.

The cathedral of St Maurice took 300 years to complete, from the 12th to the 15th centuries, and so combines characteristics of both Romanesque and Gothic styles. The apse and the vaulting are Gothic, and there are both Gothic and Romanesque historiated capitals. The cathedral is triple-naved but has no transept. The façade, with three portals is a masterpiece of the Flamboyant Gothic style with some fine carving in the upper parts of the arches and the tympana. The statues formerly at the base of the arches were removed at some time in the past. Despite some wear from centuries of weather, the façade is in good condition, and is one of the finest examples of the Gothic carving of the end of the 15th century.

The church of St Pierre, now used as an archaeological museum, is the oldest Christian monument in Vienne, and one of the oldest in France. Parts of it date from the 5th and 6th centuries, notably the north, west, and south walls. The Romanesque bell tower and porch were erected in the 12th century. There is an 11th-century statue of the patron saint of this church inside the cathedral.

In the southern part of Vienne, somewhat away from the other points of interest, there is a curious ancient

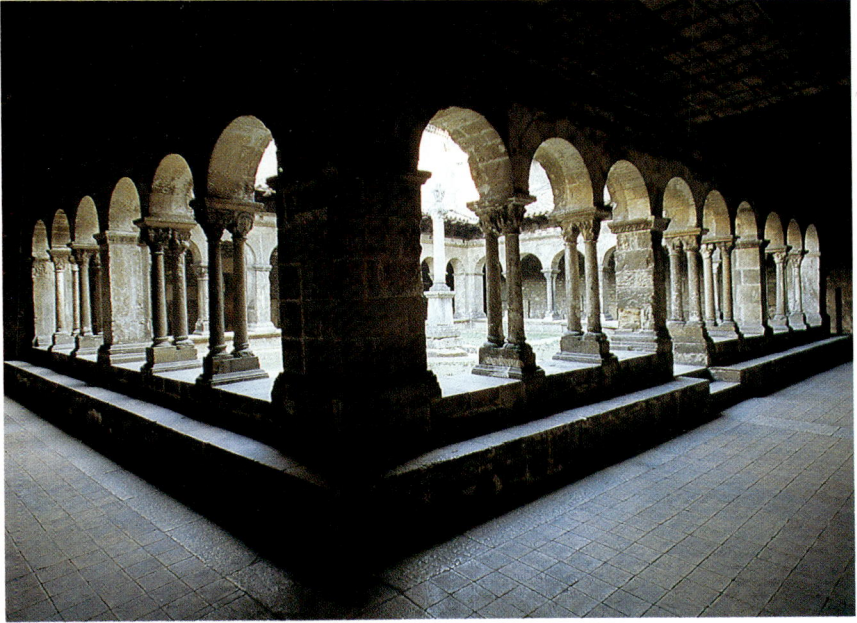

The cloister of the Romanesque church of St André-le-Bas in Vienne

structure, about 20m high, known as the Pyramid. In the Middle Ages it was thought to be the tomb of Pontius Pilate, who was believed to have left Jerusalem after the crucifixion and to have come to Vienne where, stricken with remorse, he drowned himself in the Rhône. Not a bad legend, but later scholarship asserts confidently that this clearly unfinished structure was a replacement for an obelisk which had stood in the centre of the arena of the amphitheatre and which had been destroyed in a Barbarian attack on Vienne in 275AD. Its curious appearance is said to be due to its having been started at a time when the Empire was in decline and there was neither money nor incentive to finish it. For many visitors today its

chief interest will be that it was from this monument that one of France's most renowned chefs, Fernand Point, took the name of his restaurant, which was for so many years a place of pilgrimage for gastronomes from all over Europe. Fernand Point died some years ago, and Madame Point carried on until her own death. The Pyramid Restaurant is still there in the street named after the great chef, the avenue Fernand Point, but it now belongs to a group of Paris businessmen who have completely renovated the premises. It was always very expensive and remains so, but at the time of writing it has been reopened less than a year and it is a little early to say how well it compares with its great days.

67

Gothic carving on the façade of the St Maurice Cathedral, Vienne

*The façade of Vienne's St Maurice
Cathedral includes a fine example of
Flamboyant Gothic carving around the door*

Hotels & Restaurants

Prices: A = Very Expensive, B = Expensive, C = Moderately Expensive, D = Average, E = Cheap.

AMBÉRIEUX-EN-DOMBES (01330 Ain): **Les Bichonnières**, route de Savigneux (74 00 82 07), 11km west of Villars and the bird sanctuary. A typical Logis de France with a very good regional restaurant. Pleasant, peaceful, countrified. Rooms D–E. Meals D.

LYON (69000 Rhône):

Hotels: Very wide choice at all levels but many with no restaurant. The following is a selection from those near the centre.

Cour des Loges, 6 rue du Boeuf, 69005 (78 42 75 75). One of the world's most luxurious and unusual hotels, nothing else like it anywhere. In the heart of the old Renaissance quarter. A group of 17th-century houses in Florentine style, around a courtyard, beautifully and boldy converted with the most modern techniques. Superb interior décor and furnishing. Indoor pool like a Roman bath. Ten apartments and 53 rooms. Rooms A+. Meals B.

Lyon Metropole, 85 quai Joseph Gillet, 69004 (78 29 20 20). Extraordinarily well-equipped and roomy hotel on the banks of the Saône. 15 tennis courts, 4 squash courts, Olympic swimming pool, golf practice. Rooms C. Meals C–D.

Royal, 20 pl Bellecour, 69002 (78 37 57 31). Centrally situated traditional hotel, with some modern, some period rooms. Rooms B–D. Meals D.

Mercure Pont Pasteur, 70 av Leclerc, 69007 (78 58 68 53). Large, well-equipped modern hotel. Spacious, sound-proofed rooms. Swimming pool. Rooms C. Meals D.

Bellecordière, 18 rue Bellecordière, 69002 (78 42 27 78). Newly converted small hotel near pl Bellecour. No restaurant, but wide choice nearby. Rooms D.

Phénix, 7 quai de Bondy, 69005 (78 28 30 40). Pleasant small hotel in the old quarter by the Saône. No restaurant. Rooms D–E.

Restaurants: Lyon and its region can make a strong claim to be the world's capital of fine food. There are hundreds of restaurants, 30–40 of them of the highest standards, and half a dozen among the greatest. Competition is intense, so the tourist is not likely to be disappointed by whatever takes his fancy. The following selection of the best and most characteristic is for special occasions.

Leon de Lyon, 1 rue Pléney (78 28 11 33). Near the pl des Terreaux and behind the Museum of Fine Arts. The absolute in Lyonnais cuisine, style, and personality. Very good value for the standards offered. Meals B–C.

La Mère Brazier, 12 rue Royale (78 28 15 49). Near the quai A. Lasagne (right bank of the Rhône) north of the Pont Morand. Jacotte Brazier is the best known of the *mères*, the famous women chefs of Lyon, and the third generation in this restaurant. Sixty years at the heart of the business, political and social life of Lyon is a tradition worth maintaining. Authentic and delicious Lyonnais food, superb wine list. Closed Aug. Meals B–C.

Vettard, 7 pl Bellecour (78 42 07 59). Distinguished, classical, reliable, excellent service. Closed Aug. Meals B–C.

La Tour Rose, 16 rue du Boeuf (78 37 25 90). In the heart of old Lyon in a 17th-century building. Superb food and wines, impeccable service, all rather grand. Closed two weeks in Aug. Meals B.

Orsi, 3 pl Kleber (78 89 57 68). Well established and consistent, in the best traditions of *haute cuisine*. No surprises. Meals A–B.

L'Estragon, 27 rue St Vincent (78 28 14 51). Near quai St Vincent, left bank of the Rhône. Sound, good value restaurant. Open till midnight. Meals C–D.

La Mère Vittet, 26 cours Verdun (near pl Carnot) (78 37 20 17). Big, busy, brasserie in Lyonnais style. Open 24 hours a day, but nevertheless maintains high standards of cuisine and service. Meals C–D.

LYON REGION

COLLONGES AU MONT D'OR: **Paul Bocuse**, 50 quai de la Plage (78 22 01 40), 9km north of Lyon by N51. A place of pilgrimage for lovers of fine food, where the traditional *haute cuisine* is unexcelled. The greatest of chefs, and a great 'character', Bocuse has international interests, but still maintains the highest possible standards here. Open every day. Meals: A+ and then some.

RILLEUX-LA-PAPE: **Larivoire** (78 88 50 92), 9km north of Lyon by N83. A family business where the son, Bernard Constantin, learned his art at the Savoy, then Maxim's, and then with Bocuse, before returning home to take over. Superb cooking, fine wine list, terrace overlooking the Rhône. Closed first week of Sept. Meals B–C.

PÉROUGES (01800 Meximieux, Ain): **Ostellerie du Vieux Pérouges** (74 61 00 88). One of the oldest and most attractive inns in France, in the middle of this restored medieval village. Modern comfort although some of the medieval character of the hostelry remains. Excellent regional cooking and good wines. Rooms A–B. Meals B–C.

VIENNE (38200 Isère): **Château des Sept Fontaines**, Seyssuel (74 85 25 70), 4km north-west of Vienne via N7 and D4. Old country house converted to a pleasant hotel. Park, tennis, sauna. Rooms C–D. Meals D.

La Pyramide, 14 bld Fernand Point (74 53 01 96). The restaurant founded by Fernand Point, considered by many the greatest chef of this century, still exists. Fernand Point died in 1955, and his widow continued the business for many more years. After her death the property was sold to a business syndicate, and has been renovated. Meals A+.

Le Bec Fin, 7 pl St Maurice (74 85 76 72). Charming restaurant in a fine old house opposite the cathedral. Excellent value. Meals C–D.

𝑖

VILLARS-LES-DOMBES (01330 Ain): **Auberge des Chasseurs**, Bouligneux (74 98 10 02), 4km from Villars-les-Dombes via the D2. Very good country restaurant, using local produce, including game in season. Closed last fortnight of Aug. Meals C–D.
La Table des Etangs, Le Plantay (74 98 15 31), 5km north-east of Villars via N83 and D70. Above average village restaurant. Meals C–D.

Museums etc: opening times

Note: am/pm means closed for lunch, normally for two hours.

LYON: Roman Theatres, 1 March to 31 October, Mon–Sat, am/pm. Sun pm. Rest of the year am/pm Mon–Fri.
Gallo-Roman Museum, am/pm, closed Mon and Tue.
Museum of Fine Arts, daily 10.45 to 18.00, except Tue.
Historical Museum of Fabrics and **Museum of Decorative Arts**, one ticket for both, am/pm, closed Mon and public holidays.
Museum of Printing and Banking, am/pm, closed Mon, Tue and public holidays.

ROCHETAILLÉE: Vintage Car Museum, daily am/pm.

VIENNE: Roman theatre, am/pm, closed Mon, Tue and Sun am. One ticket admits to Roman theatre, cloister of St André-le-Bas, Musée St Pierre, and the Museum of Fine Arts.

Leisure and Night Life

In common with all large French cities, Lyon offers every conceivable form of night life, from smart night clubs, to discos, old time dancing clubs, gay clubs, and seedy pick-up bars. Those who read French will find Le Guide de la Nuit, Lyon Poche, a comprehensive and useful guide which includes hotels and restaurants as well as night life. Hotel porters can often help with a suitable choice.

L'ALIBI, 13 quai Roman Rolland, Lyon 5. Straightforward, roomy disco. Music varied. Right of admission reserved. Open every night.

ACTUEL, 30 bld Eugene Deruel, Lyon 3. Large well-run disco. Right of admission reserved. Closed Sun, Mon, Tue.

L'ETINCELLE, 16 rue Casimir Perier, Lyon 2. Latin American, foxtrot, waltz, rock, twist. Stylish, good for keen dancers. Right of admission reserved, e.g. no jeans or sneakers.

RIVER CRUISES Boat trips of all kinds are available on the Rhône and the Saône from Lyon. They vary from 90-minute trips through the city with commentary, to longer trips with lunch or dinner on board, to cruises of up to 8 days (to the Mediterranean) on luxury hotel boats. Details from Naviginter, 3 rue de l'Arbre Sec, 69001, Lyon (78 27 78 02), or from the Office de Tourisme.

Tourist Information Offices

LYON – pl Bellecour (78 42 25 75). Will change money, and make hotel reservations but not more than five days in advance.

VIENNE – 3 cours Brillier (74 85 12 62).

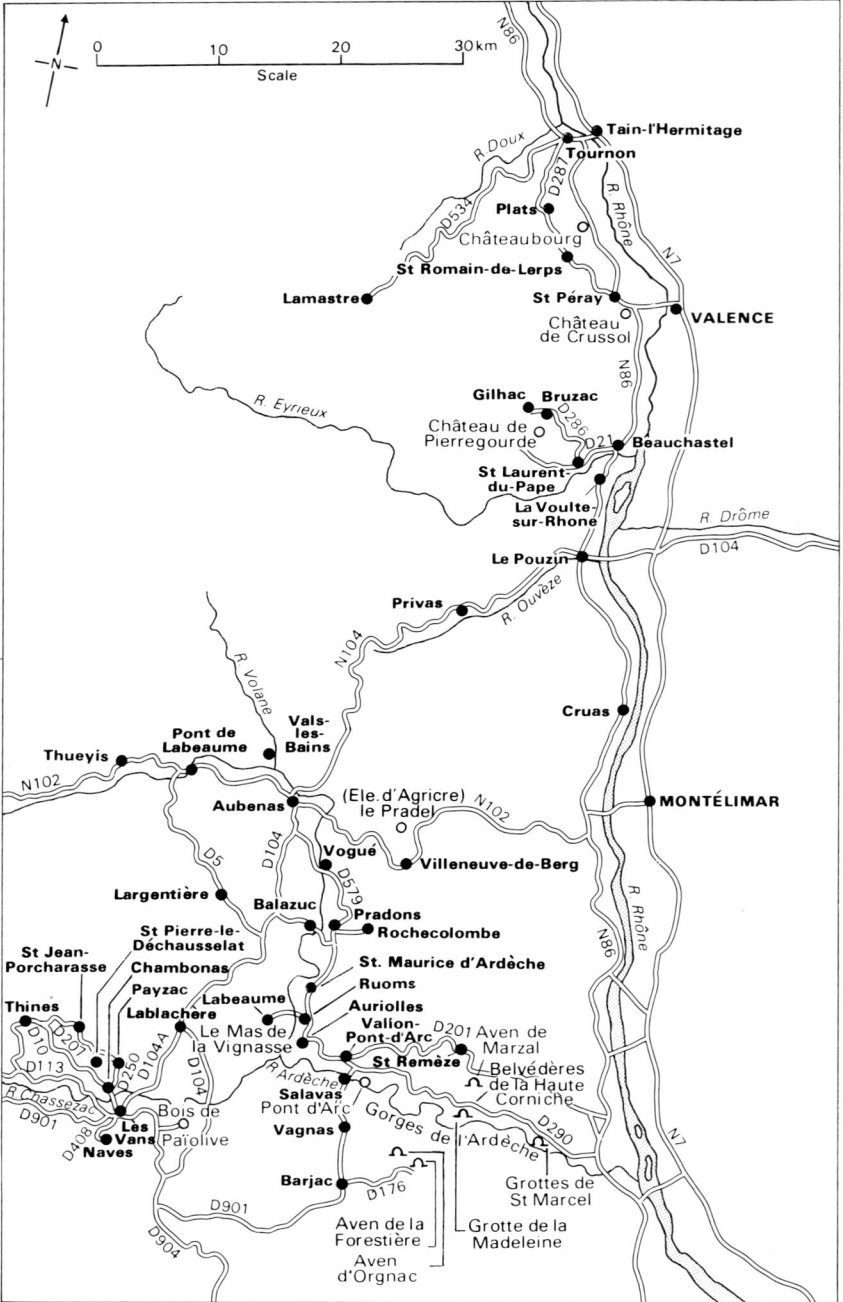

N

0 10 20 30 km

Scale

R. Doux

N86

D281

D534

R. Rhône

N7

Tain-l'Hermitage

Tournon

Plats

Châteaubourg

St Romain-de-Lerps

Lamastre

St Péray

VALENCE

Château
de Crussol

N86

R. Eyrieux

Gilhac **Bruzac**

Château de
Pierregourde

D286

D21

Beauchastel

**St Laurent-
du-Pape**

**La Voulte-
sur-Rhone**

R. Drôme

Le Pouzin

D104

Privas

R. Ouvèze

N104

R. Volane

Cruas

Thueyis

**Pont de
Labeaume**

**Vals-
les-
Bains**

N102

Aubenas

(Ele. d'Agricre)
le Pradel

N102

MONTÉLIMAR

D5

D104

Vogué

Villeneuve-de-Berg

Largentière

Balazuc

D579

Pradons
Rochecolombe

**St Pierre-le-
Déchausselat**

**St Jean-
Porcharasse**

Chambonas

Payzac

Labeaume

St. Maurice d'Ardèche

Ruoms

Auriolles

Thines

Lablachère

**Le Mas de
la Vignasse**

**Valion-
Pont-d'Arc**

D201

Aven de
Marzal

St Remèze

D10

D207

D250

D104A

D104

R. Ardèche

Salavas
Pont d'Arc

Belvédères
de la Haute
Corniche

R. Chassezac

**Bois de
Païolive**

Gorges de l'Ardèche

D290

N7

D113

**Les
Vans**

Naves

D408

D901

Vagnas

Grottes de
St Marcel

Barjac

D176

D901

Aven de la
Forestière

Grotte de la
Madeleine

D904

Aven
d'Orgnac

R. Rhône

N86

74

6
Ardèche

It is a good idea to cross to the west bank of the Rhône at Vienne and to continue towards Tournon on the N86 via Condrieu and Serrières. Though neither of these towns have any great interest for the modern visitor, they do have a place in the history of the Rhône. In the days before the coming of steam tugs and barges **Condrieu** was the chief base of the tough sailors who formed the barge crews, and it is one of the places where the river traditions of the past are kept up. Jousting tournaments in boats are held on the first Sunday in July. **Serrières** is another town which was famous for its sailors and preserves its past in the Museum of the Boatmen of the Rhône, which is installed in the 13th-century chapel of St Sornin, just south of the town. Here you can see clothes, tools, and equipment used by the sailors, and there are several examples of the mariner's cross, which the captain placed at the front of his vessel to protect it from the dangers of the voyage.

There is an exhibit in this museum which should appeal to lovers of horror films and others who like a touch of the gruesome. In the loft above the choir there is an ossuary containing more than 350 skeletons, four of them mummified and in an upright position. They are known locally as the *mandulons*, but no one seems to know for sure why they are there. They are believed to be about 300 years old, and it is supposed that at that time it was planned to move the cemetery of St Sornin, perhaps because it was repeatedly flooded by the Rhône. The bodies were removed from the graves to await reburial, and at this point, perhaps, bureaucracy intervened.

From Serrières the N86 runs due south parallel with the Rhône and often right next to it. The few small towns and villages along this road are in the department of Ardèche but not of it. The real Ardèche is just up there on your right, little known, mysterious, hard to get at beyond the barrier of hills rising, often like a cliff, from the river valley. The few roads that lead off to the right all climb more than 300m in the first few kilometres, and once up there you have arrived in the true Ardèche, one of the loneliest, wildest and most beautiful departments in the whole of France. Here there are no large towns, no railways, few buses, only two roads important enough to have N numbers. The further you go west the higher the land becomes. The whole of it, the Vivarais mountains, the high plateau and other

mountain groups, all form part of the western slopes of the Massif Central, and the whole of Ardèche is tilted from west to east towards the Rhône.

In this rugged country of mountains and moorland there are occasional forests and lakes, but great stretches of upland are rocky and infertile, treeless, covered only in low scrub. The land is watered by dozens of crystal trout streams and impetuous rivers with splendid gorges and waterfalls. It is a region of savage extremes of climate. In winter the higher slopes are held fast in snow. In summer the sun scorches the plateau, and in the valleys the heat is all-pervading. Those lovely rivers, in summer so full of charm and innocence, can at any time from early autumn to the end of spring flood with dangerous suddenness and ferocity.

Over the centuries this hard land has bred a people of fierce and independent spirit. But the population has been falling for many years, as the young have left to seek a better fortune elsewhere. Those who have stayed, in spite of the difficulties, have done so because in the few places where the land is fertile it will grow anything. They say that every fruit known to France, from the apple to the fig, thrives somewhere in Ardèche. Another old saying is that Ardèche is a region which has something of everything, but not much. What it does have for the summer visitor is the great outdoors in beauty and unconfined variety. This is where you can fish in streams where trout are counted by the hundred, where you can walk endless miles through glorious scenery

The Eyrieux river follows a path between steep gorges

on national footpaths (GR7, GR4, GR420), where you can ride through valleys and over hills on 160km of pony trails, with accommodation for horse and rider every night, where you can canoe or kayak on rivers of every level of difficulty. Some more unusual holiday activities available in Ardèche include rock climbing, cross-country cycling on mountain bikes, and off-road motoring in four-wheel-drive vehicles. Perhaps most unusual of all, a week-long break picking and classifying, under the guidance of a university professor, some of the 400 species of mushrooms found in Ardèche.

But Ardèche also has its historical and cultural side. The first charter of the old city of **Tournon**, on the N86 33km south of Serrières, was granted in 1111. It has a 15th-century château built on a rock beside the river, which houses a museum devoted to the history of Tournon and the Rhône, but more impressive for most visitors are the terraces of the château overlooking the Rhône. The upper terrace is arranged as a sort of hanging garden and has a fine view of the river. The more spacious lower terrace has a view of the town, and across the river to the vineyard slopes of Hermitage, with the heights of the plateau of Vercors in the background.

In 1536, the Dauphin of France, the son of François I and heir to the throne, died in this castle. According to rumour he was poisoned by his equerry.

The imposing church of St Julien has a Flamboyant Gothic façade, with a square 17th-century bell tower beside it. The roomy interior has a triple nave, and there is an unusual coffered ceiling in wood. In the

Penitents' Chapel there are some 15th-century frescoes, and in another chapel there is a Resurrection, painted in 1576 by Jean Capassin, a pupil of Raphael. There is also a 17th-century organ, restored some years ago.

The only passenger train in Ardèche runs from Tournon the 33km to **Lamastre**. It runs only in summer, as a tourist attraction. It is a narrow-gauge railway, with steam engine and stock from the beginning of this century. The train leaves Tournon at 10.00 and arrives back at 18.00. On its two-hour journey it follows the valley of the Doux through lovely scenery and passes through two gorges thickly wooded with oaks, holm oaks, stunted pines, bracken and broom. The excursion allows time for a leisurely lunch in the well-known Barratero Restaurant in Lamastre, or one of the others in the town, or more modestly, a picnic in the quiet Segnobos Park, where you are unlikely to be disturbed.

Lamastre can also be reached by car, via the D534, a pretty road part of which is a corniche above the Gorges du Doux.

Immediately across the river from Tournon is its sister town of Tain-l'Hermitage, famous for its vineyards which produce both red and white Hermitage wines, one of the best of the Côtes du Rhône.

From Tournon a narrow road, which is also part of the GR42 national footpath, leads via the hamlets of

These little chapels are characteristic of the vineyards of Tain l'Hermitage; the village itself can be seen in the distance

A 19th-century Genius

In the early 19th century one man completely changed the everyday life of the towns of the Rhône Valley. Marc Seguin was born in 1786 at Annonay in Ardèche, and became one of the century's great innovative engineers. He was the oldest of five brothers who, it was said at the time, worked together like the fingers of one hand.

In 1826 he built the first railway in France, linking Lyon to St Etienne, 58km away, four years before Liverpool and Manchester were joined by the first British railway. In 1828 he patented a new form of tubular boiler, enabling steam engines to travel much faster than before. He gave his patent rights for this boiler into the public domain, not wishing, he said, 'to make a personal benefit from the intelligence which Heaven gave me'.

But Seguin's biggest achievement was in bridge-building. He was the first person to think of using cables of interwoven steel wire in building suspension bridges. Although the principle of suspension bridges was known to antiquity, the ropes and chains of earlier designs were not always safe. Seguin tested his theories by building a small bridge across the Cance in his home town of Annonay, and then a somewhat larger one across the Galaure, near St Vallier, in Drôme. The success of these constructions led to an official invitation to build one of these new-style bridges across the Rhône – at his own expense, of course.

Despite the unfamiliar problems in a construction of the required size, Seguin accepted the challenge. The bridge between Tournon and Tain l'Hermitage was started in May 1824 and opened on 15 August 1825. Seguin was allowed to make it a toll bridge, and he recovered his costs many times over. The bridge remained in use for 140 years, although a second bridge was built at Tournon in 1846.

Seguin's bridge marked the end of the Rhône as a barrier between east and west. By the middle of the century another 20 suspension bridges had been put across the river. Greatly improved communications threatened the livelihood of the professional sailors and barge owners and Seguin was often threatened with violence and narrowly escaped being thrown off one of his bridges. But Seguin and his brothers went on to build 186 suspension bridges in France and abroad.

The private life of this extraordinary man was as prolific and daring as his professional life. At 24 he married Augustine Duret d'Annonay, who bore him 13 children. At 53, after Augustine's death, he married his 20-year-old niece, Augustine Montgolfier, who bore him six more children. Between the oldest and the youngest of his children there was a difference of 47 years.

Plats and St Romain-de-Lerps to St Péray. This is a route worth taking for its spectacular views. At **St Romain-de-Lerps**, near the old tower and on either side of a small chapel, there are observation platforms and an orientation table. The panorama extends over 13 departments. The heights of the plateau of Vercors can be seen to the east, and beyond them the snow-capped peaks of the Mont Blanc Massif and the Alps. To the west there are the summits of the Vivarais mountains, dominated by Mont Mézenc, and to the south Mont Ventoux is easily picked out.

As you descend towards the wine-producing village of St Péray on the D287 there are more fine views over the Rhône Valley and the Valence area, and ahead the romantic ruins of the **Château de Crussol**, perched on the edge of a limestone cliff 240m above the Rhône. A huge, ugly and unmissable white statue of the Virgin looks down on St Péray, and gives a stony benediction to the vineyards, the village and the valley. If you want to visit the ruins of the Château de Crussol, take the road that leads to the statue and park the car just behind it. From this point it is about half an hour's energetic walk up to the ruins. They really are an impressive sight. The castle was built in the 12th century by one of the Seigneurs de Crussol. Through judicious marriages and service as courtiers to a succession of kings from Louis XI onwards, the lords of Crussol enjoyed fame and fortune for more than 300 years. Towards the end of the 16th century the castle was partly destroyed by fire, and it was further destroyed during the religious wars of the 17th century, and afterwards fell into ruin. There

The Château de Crussol stands on a breathtaking site, overlooking the Rhône

is a tradition that Napoleon, when he was a young soldier stationed at Valence just across the Rhône, frequently visited the ruins, and that on one occasion in 1785 he and his brother Joseph risked their lives by climbing up to the castle via the cliff face. In addition to its history, the mountain of Crussol is of particular interest to geologists, as several layers of different sedimentary rocks can be clearly made out. Stone from this mountain was used to construct the amphitheatre of Arles in Roman times, and it was often used for the construction of public buildings in the Vivarais and in Valence, and for the pillars of the Palace of Justice in Lyon.

Another magnificently sited ruined castle worth a visit is the **Château de Pierregourde**. To reach it continue south on the N86 from St Péray, and at the villae of Beauchastel turn right on to the D21 for St Laurent-du-Pape. The valley of the river Eyrieux here, just before it joins the Rhône, is a

The ruins of Château Pierregourde magnificently sited above the Eyrieux valley

wonderful sight in spring, when the extensive peach orchards seem to be awash with bright pink blossom. These orchards produce some of the world's finest peaches – and a lot of them, an average of 16,000 tons per year. In the centre of St Laurent turn right on to the narrow road signposted to Gilhac and Bruzac. It starts to climb at once into a barren and rocky landscape, twisting and turning, and with some splendid views. Then you see ahead of you the imposing ruins of the château, which is known to have existed in 1217. An unmade track leads to it and it is advisable to walk the last few hundred metres. As you explore the ruins you will find a rocky platform with grand views across the Rhône to the whole of the department

of Drôme and the far-off Alps. Further to the south Mont Ventoux stands out clearly, and to the west across the tangled hills of the Vivarais is the summit of Mont Mézenc. The views are better in the afternoon light than in the glare of a summer morning.

During the religious wars in the 16th century the lords of Pierregourde took the side of the Protestants and in 1568 the last of them was killed fighting with the Protestant army. As many of the local villages were strongly Protestant, Cardinal Richelieu had the castle destroyed in 1630, along with many others throughout France, to prevent it being used as a base against the Catholics. Keen walkers may like to know that the Château de Pierregourde can be reached from St

81

Laurent-du-Pape by the national foot-path GR42, a distance of about 6km.

Continue south on the N86 via La Voulte-sur-Rhône and Le Pouzin, neither of which is of particular interest to the tourist. But Le Pouzin was the port for Privas, once the Huguenot capital of Ardèche and now the prefecture, and the N104 turns off here through the valley of the Ouvèze to Privas, climbing throughout the 14km and giving those motorists who have not previously ventured off the N86 a foretaste of the superb upland scenery of the heart of Ardèche.

Those visitors interested in Romanesque churches may like, before taking the road to Privas, to carry on down the N86 to **Cruas**, where there is a really splendid abbey church, the only one remaining of four once established in the Vivarais, and all that is left of the abbey founded in Cruas in the 9th century. This little town is an interesting example of the contrasting worlds of the Rhône Valley. Its old stone houses huddle around the great church and the fortifications of the old château, and all is covered with a fine white dust from a large cement works by the river, and not far away the great towers of the nuclear power station of Cruas-Meysse pour forth great clouds of smoke. The building of this power station was bitterly contested, and for good reasons. The land around Cruas is the thinnest part of the Earth's crust in France, and is subject to frequent movements, which might or might not become more serious. Moreover, at the time the site was first-class agricultural land, and also the prevailing winds blow the smoke directly over the towns of Le Teil and Montélimar.

The abbey church at Cruas, founded by Benedictines in AD804

But in the end the authorities, as always, were the winners.

None of this detracts from the interest of the church itself, first consecrated by Pope Urban II in 1095. The façade is dominated by a square tower, but the tower which rises from the middle of the transept is circular and carries a conical spire. There are some good capitals in the 11th-century crypt, and there is an unusual mosaic in Byzantine style and said to date from 1098 in the choir.

The 'castle' in the upper part of the town really consists of a group of fortifications around a 12th-century chapel, and was built by the monks of the abbey in the 14th century to provide a refuge in times of danger.

Privas is a charming and lively little town situated in a bowl among the mountains, with seven hills of its own, three rivers and seven bridges. Not much remains of its historical past except for an old tower, called the Diane de Poitiers tower, after the *douce amie* of Henri II, who was the suzerain of Privas from 1547. The reason that so little remains of the old Privas, as compared with many similar towns, is that Privas was a Protestant town, and its people fought fiercely against the Catholics throughout the religious wars, until it was recognised by Henri IV as a stronghold of Protestantism in the Edict of Nantes in 1598. History might have been kind to Privas but when the local Protestant

A Huguenot Family

During the Wars of Religion the town of Privas was one of the strongholds of the Protestant faith. About 15km to the north via the D2 and the D344, at Le Bouschet de Pranles, a farmhouse has been turned into a small museum of Protestantism. The house itself is interesting as a fine example of the stone-built, fortified farmhouse with an enclosed courtyard, as built in the Vivarais in the 15th and 16th centuries.

It has been made a museum because it was the birthplace of two Protestant martyrs, Pierre and Marie Durand. Their father, Etienne, had been converted to the new faith, and in 1726 his son, Pierre, became a clandestine priest. His tireless preaching of the reformed religion aroused the anger of the authorities. His mother, father, and young sister, Marie, were arrested and imprisoned. Marie was 15 years old and was shut up in the Tour de Constance at Aigues-Mortes in 1730. She was repeatedly offered her freedom, if she would renounce her religion. She steadfastly refused, and it was 38 years before she was released. Her brother, Pierre, had been executed at Montpellier in 1732.

The house has a priest's hole in the kitchen chimney, and there are souvenirs of the Durand family. Every Whit Monday there is a Protestant gathering at Pranles.

Museum opening times: am/pm every day except Sun, 15 June to 15 September, Sat and Sun afternoons, Easter to June, and 15 September to 1 November.

leader died, his widow Paule de Chambaud, had two suitors for remarriage, one Protestant and one Catholic. Apparently she considered some other qualities more important than religious attachment, because she chose the younger suitor, who was a Catholic. This infuriated the townspeople, who did not want a Catholic as their lord and master. They attacked and partially destroyed his castle. A few years later Cardinal Richelieu and King Louis XIII brought an army of 20,000 men and besieged Privas. The defenders, who numbered only 1,600, withstood the siege for more than two weeks, but then the town was taken by storm, pillaged and burned, and its inhabitants massacred.

Today Privas is a quiet little administrative town with a few small industries. It is the capital of *marrons glacés*, the succulent sweetmeats made from the fruit of the Spanish chestnut tree which grows in many parts of Ardèche. As in the neighbouring Cévennes, the chestnut tree has always been important to the economy of the Ardèche. Its wood, which resists decay from water for many years, was for this reason much used for the windows, exterior doors and roof beams of houses, where it had the additional advantage of being repellent to spiders. It was also used for fence posts, stakes for vineyards and gardens, and hoops for wine barrels, and was also made into charcoal. In hard times the chestnuts themselves were ground into flour from which a kind of coarse bread was made. The tree was often called 'the bread tree' in the Cévennes and Ardèche.

Pleasant though it is, Privas is not a place that need detain the tourist for long, and it is rather short of restaurants and hotel accommodation. Those looking for somewhere to eat or to stay would do better to continue the 30-odd kilometres along the N104 to the little spa town of Vals-les-Bains, which has no less than eight Logis de France, or its next-door neighbour Aubenas, which has a Logis and an Auberge de France.

Vals-les-Bains is situated in the valley of the Volane, one of those burbling little rivers which can occasionally suddenly lose its temper with drastic results. The town follows the valley, and is long and narrow, nowhere more than 300m wide and about 2km long. The French take their spas with a degree of seriousness which has not been felt for English spas since the Romans left Bath.

There are many of these small thermal resorts, as well as some big ones, in and around the Massif Central, and Vals-les-Bains is one of the most attractive of them. It is one of the few spas of southern France which was not discovered and exploited by the Romans. It first became known in the 17th century when a local politician, a M. Expilly, was cured of gall-stones by drinking the waters. But it was at the end of the 19th century that it reached the height of its popularity. It was one of the gems of the *belle époque*, and today, with its charming parks with spreading cedars and giant sequoias, its period villas, its gracious public buildings and cheerful river, it still has an unpretentious if slightly faded air of genuine style about it. There are no less than 150 springs in the valley, all but two of them cold, and the water, which contains bicarbonate of soda and other minerals, is said to be effective in the treatment of digestive troubles, diabetes, and rheumatism.

The essence of the cure is drinking the water, and resting. In one of the parks there is something quite rare in France, a spring which is a natural geyser and shoots a column of water 8m into the air at six-hour intervals, 11.30 and 17.30 (summer time).

For visitors who want to make a short stay in Ardèche there is no better base than Vals-les-Bains, which is near the heart of Ardèche, with excursions possible in all directions, and a good choice of hotels and restaurants. Its holiday amenities include an Olympic swimming pool, tennis courts, mini-golf, and a casino, theatre, cinema and night club.

From Vals-les-Bains you can take the N102 the few kilometres south to **Aubenas**, a pleasant town situated on a cliff with its back to the northern hills and looking full south down the valley of the Ardèche. With its red Roman tiled roofs it already has some of the allure of Provence. The old part of the town, with its narrow streets and a number of old mansions, is worth strolling round, and the castle is unusual and attractive. Its roofs of multi-coloured glazed tiles look new but in fact are 18th-century. The oldest part of the castle, which now includes the Town Hall, is the 12th-century keep, which is a good deal higher than the round towers on either side of the façade.

The roads of Ardèche in general and in particular in the western heights are consistently spectacular but, as they follow the tangled contours of the country, it is difficult to estimate how long any drive taking in several destinations might take. Out and back excursions are usually more practical.

The Pont du Diable crosses the Ardèche at Thueyis, 10km west of Vals-les-Bains

Greenfingers

Olivier de Serres was a gentleman farmer, a writer, and a Huguenot. He was born at Villeneuve-de-Berg in Ardèche in 1539, and died at his country estate at Le Pradel, 7km north of Villeneuve, in 1619.

When King Henri IV asked for ideas to help restore the economy after the Wars of Religion, de Serres offered an essay on the possibilities of silk farming. King Henri liked the idea and set an example by planting 20,000 mulberry trees in the Tuileries in Paris. A silk industry grew up and France became an exporter instead of an importer of luxury fabrics.

In 1600 Olivier de Serres published a huge volume called *Le Théâtre de l'Agriculture et Mesnage des Champs* (*The Realm of Agriculture and the Management of Land*). It was not only a beautifully written work, it was also full of practical ideas, new at the time. He advised deep ploughing, the rotation of crops, the spraying of vines against disease, and the cultivation of unfamiliar crops. On his own farm at Pradel he introduced the culture of maize, sugar beet, hops, potatoes, and almonds, all to become commonplace in France. Not for nothing is he known as the father of French agriculture. Henri IV loved de Serres's book, not only for its charm and style, but for the author's serene philosophy and deep knowledge of people as well as plants. He had it read to him every night after dinner, over four months. Since its publication the book has run to over 20 editions, and is still a classic.

The farm at Pradel is now a school of agriculture.

Several such excursions are possible from Vals-les-Bains or Aubenas. For those with an interest in gardening or agriculture, a trip to Le Pradel (take the N102 from Aubenas to Villeneuve-du-Berg, then the D258 for 5km to the north) is well worthwhile (see Box on 'Greenfingers', p. 86).

Gorges de l'Ardèche

Take the D579 south from Aubenas to Vogüé, and continue on through the valley of the Ardèche via Pradons and Ruoms, where you turn off for Vallon-Pont-d'Arc and the gorges. But this part of Ardèche has a number of ancient and picturesque villages which repay visiting.

It is worth stopping off at the village of **Vogüé** to have a look at the castle, the ancestral home of one of France's best-known families, long distinguished in French history, and still known today for the champagne and superb burgundies (Bonnes Mares) produced by some members of the family. The village stands between the Ardèche and a great limestone cliff, from which the houses and even the castle itself, all built in the same stone, seem to have fallen like great boulders.

The castle dates from the 12th century but was completely rebuilt in the 17th when it was bought by Melchior de Vogüé. At the time of the Revolution the castle was sold off as a national asset, but the family were able to buy it back in 1840 and it still belongs to them today. In addition to the interesting interior, which includes a monumental staircase and an impressive state room in which the meetings of the Council of Languedoc were held for many years, there are some attractive hanging gardens on the eastern side of the castle, from which there are views over the village and down the valley of the Ardèche.

The Vogüé family were originally, in feudal times, the lords of another village, **Rochecolombe**, a few kilometres away. Apart from the Romanesque chapel, which served as a parish church until the 19th century and was kept in good condition, this ancient village with a ruined tower as a landmark, is itself a picturesque ruin. Fifteen generations of Vogüés are buried in the mausoleum of the chapel; the last of them was buried there in the 16th century. The most interesting items from the chapel were taken away a few years ago and placed for safekeeping in the chapel of the castle.

One summer day 25 years ago the family held a reunion in this old village where their long history began. A hundred and ninety of them attended, coming from every part of France. To reach Rochecolombe turn left off the D579 in the village of St Maurice-d'Ardèche on to the D401, and do not be surprised when, after a few kilometres, you arrive in what appears to be a fairly modern village. The old feudal village is another 15 minutes' walk along a track beside the stream.

Vogüé, though perhaps not of outstanding interest, is a classic example of an important facet of French life and history – the long association of a particular family with a particular place. The way in which a town or a district has been used as a springboard

to national power is characteristic of France, even today. In the past it was the nobles in their strongholds who gradually extended their influence by battle, marriage alliances or service to the monarchy or Church. Today all the major figures of French politics have a stronghold, a power base, a town of which they are the mayor.

Another very picturesque and ancient village, still inhabited, is only a few kilometres away on the other side of the D579. Three kilometres south of St Maurice-d'Ardèche the D294 on the right leads to **Balazuc**, a 12th-century village, nestled against the cliff in a secluded gorge. It is a pleasant walk upstream along the right bank beside the Ardèche, and as you climb away from the village there are several places with good views. As you look back it is easy to imagine how utterly remote it must have been 1,000 years ago, and to believe the local tradition that its first inhabitants were Moorish survivors of the invading Saracen army defeated by Charles Martel near the Dordogne river about 735AD.

The next village down the D579 is **Ruoms**, and on the way the river has cut a deep gorge, and the road beside the river is sometimes in short tunnels cut through the rock. Ruoms itself has a clearly defined old quarter within ramparts with seven towers. It is at Ruoms that you turn off towards Vallon-Pont-d'Arc and the Gorges de l'Ardèche but unless you are in a rush there are two other places nearby worth visiting.

Only 3½km away, **Labeaume** is a lovely old village at the entry to the Gorge de la Beaume, a tributary of the Ardèche. With its ancient houses and its narrow alleys, some of them roofed over, it is full of attractive corners for the artist and photographer. It is another place where it is possible to enjoy a walk along the gorge opposite worn cliffs eroded into fantastic shapes by the torrent.

A few minutes' walk across country from Labeaume, or more lazily by car to the village of Auriolles and then an even shorter walk, is **Le Mas de la Vignasse**, an interesting site for those interested in the work of Alphonse Daudet, author of *Lettres de Mon Moulin*.

It was on this farm that Alphonse Daudet's mother was brought up. Her parents were farmers specialising in the production of raw silk, and it was here, while visiting his grandparents, that the 18-year-old Daudet fell in love with his pretty cousin, Marie Reynaud, and began his writing career with poems about their affair, *Les Amoureuses*.

The farm, dilapidated almost to the point of ruin, was bought in 1937 by M. Roger Ferlet, who restored the old house, dating from 1515, and gradually made the whole property a fascinating museum of silk culture and general farming as it was in the Vivarais between 1750 and 1850, together with a literary museum of Alphonse Daudet's life and works. The beauty of this place is that it is a restoration on the spot, not a reconstruction in some alien place.

Everything is there, just where it would have been 200 years ago. The kitchen, with its furniture, its pots and pans around the fireplace, is the kitchen as it once was. The key elements of farm life of that period are all there: a weaver's loom from the Renaissance, the cupboards in which the daughter of the house would have built up and stored her trousseau, all the tools and equipment required for the production of silk, the implements necessary for the more general work of the farm, even the harness for the mules. All this alone is of considerable historical and social interest, but there is also the almost tangible presence of Daudet himself, in dozens of family photographs, letters, and other souvenirs, as well as first editions of his books. Altogether it is a strong evocation of life in Ardèche more than 100 years ago, and of one life in particular.

Return to Ruoms, and just south of the village, turn left (the road is still the D579) for Vallon-Pont-d'Arc. There is no need to go into the town itself; it is of little interest, unless you want to buy something for a picnic lunch. If not, turn right before you reach the town, where Pont d'Arc and the Gorges de l'Ardèche are signposted. This road brings you after 5km to **Pont d'Arc**.

It is a good idea to park the car, and go down to the river on foot to take a close look at this impressive natural wonder, which forms a bridge over the river 34m high and 59m across at water level. The road actually follows the old course of the river, which swept round in a bend at this point. But at some time in the distant past some of the water took a subterranean short cut and gradually wore a tunnel through the limestone cliff, a hole which over countless centuries became steadily larger. Then during a period of flood the main course of the river abandoned its old bed and switched itself through this tunnel, enlarging it still further until the natural bridge was formed.

The natural bridge at Pont d'Arc arches 34m above the fast-flowing Ardèche

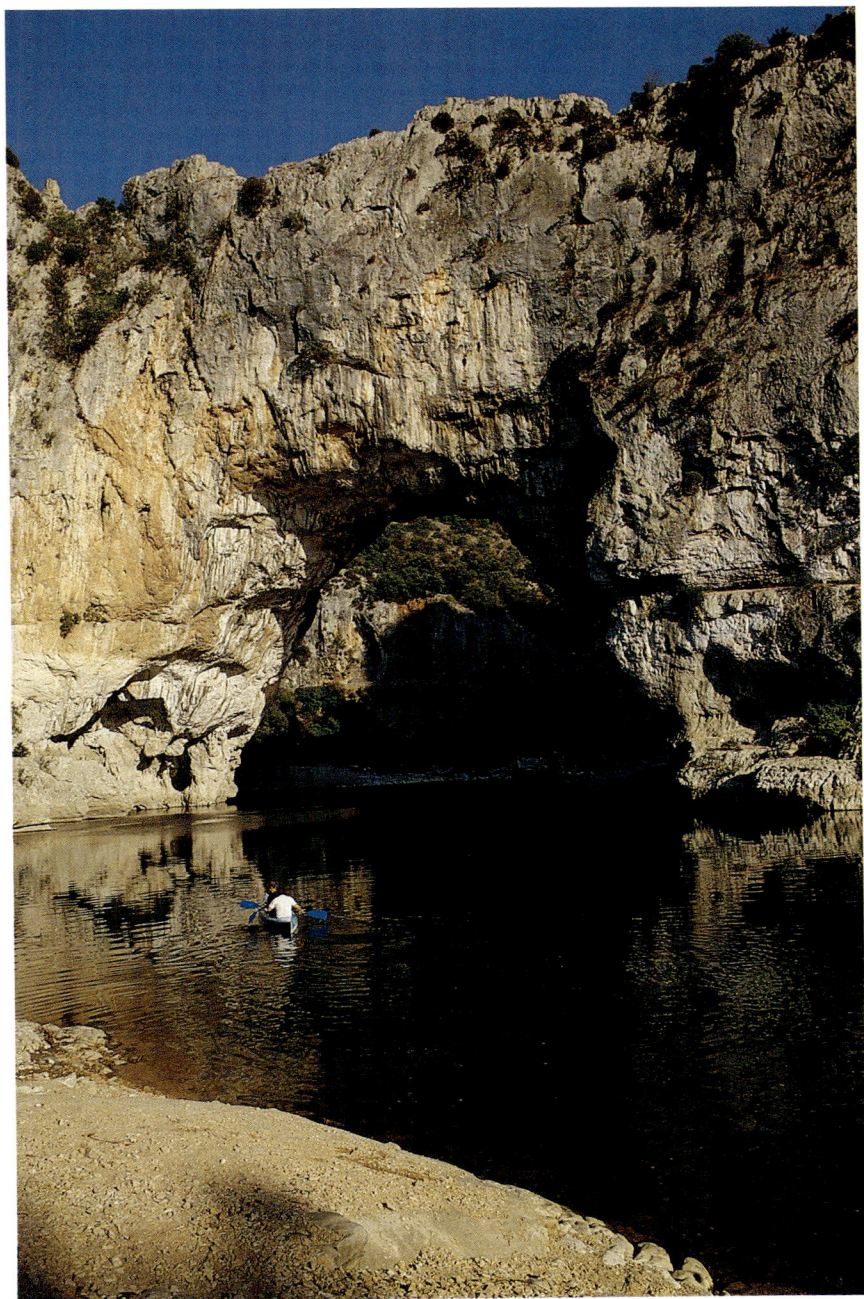

Though not on the scale of the Gorges du Tarn, which begin 80km away in the Cévennes, the **Gorges de l'Ardèche**, 30km long and with multi-coloured cliffs in places nearly 300m high, are nevertheless one of the great scenic wonders of France, and since the road runs along the top edge of the gorge, they are a great deal easier to see than the Gorges du Tarn. From Pont d'Arc itself the road, the D290, climbs to the top of the gorge and runs along the whole length of it, following every twist and turn, and with no less than twelve belvederes. The first of these, the Belvédère du Serre de Tourre is almost 200m vertically above the river and gives a superb view of the Pas de Mousse loop in the gorge. Another one especially worth stopping at is the Belvédère de Gournier, which looks down on a lovely stretch of the gorge, with a ruined farmhouse beside a small field on the opposite side of the river. From this point on, on the section of the road called the Haute Corniche, one spectacular view succeeds another every few hundred metres.

Underground Ardèche

It is a commonplace of geology that wherever there are gorges there are likely to be subterranean rivers, potholes, and cave systems, and Ardèche is no exception to this general rule. The best of these underground marvels are situated in the southern part of

The gorge of the Ardèche seen from one of the belvederes of the Haute Corniche

the department not far from the gorge. The most impressive is the **Aven d'Orgnac**. *Aven* is the word for a pothole, that is a cave or cave system with an opening in the roof, often quite small. The Aven d'Orgnac is south of the Gorges de l'Ardèche, and is most conveniently reached from Vallon-Pont-d'Arc via the D579 to Salavas, Vagnas and Barjac, where you turn left on to the D176, which brings you after 8km to the Aven d'Orgnac. It was known to the local inhabitants, who often lost sheep and goats which fell into it, but the first full exploration, by the speleologist, Robert de Joly, was not until 1935.

Although the part which has been equipped and opened to the public is remarkable for its great size, 125m wide by 250m long, and up to 40m high, it represents only about one-fifth of an enormous system, which was further explored in 1965 and 1966.

It has many stalagmites of considerable size, and originally there were many even bigger, often 25m high and from 3 to 10m thick. These crashed down during two earthquakes in the distant past, however, so long ago that new stalagmites, which grow only 2 or 3cm every hundred years, have had time to develop to great size on the ruins of the old. One of these in the central hall is no less than 50m high, and as it is roughly in the form of a cross, it is known as the Calvaire Breton. Further down into the system there are three more caves known as the Red Halls. The first of them is 96m in height, and has a kind of entry porch on natural pillars 17m high. The red colour in these caves is due to ferrous oxides which have stained the white limestone, and it is found in the walls, the columns and

Dramatic natural sculptures in the caves at Aven d'Orgnac

the roofs, and everywhere the small crystals known as 'cave pearls' gleam in the reddish light. The people who fit out caves and open them to the public cannot resist giving names to the various strange rock formations found in them. 'The forest', 'the organ pipes', 'the pulpit', 'the pine cone' and others crop up repeatedly. It sometimes requires a real effort of imagination to see the object named. In the first chamber of Orgnac there is a large stalagmite with a pronounced lean, not surprisingly called 'Pisa'. In the third Red Hall there is a so-called 'phantom ship', which some visitors may feel is more phantom than ship. But these cliché names do nothing to detract from the wonders of this underground world of stony fantasies, where in places the floor glistens like a carpet of jewels, and where centuries of water dripping through the red silence produces only an infinitesimal change. A lift takes you easily back to the surface, where there is an interesting museum illustrating the various eras of prehistory in Ardèche. Part of the Orgnac system is believed to have been inhabited by man as long as 300,000 years ago. In the grounds around the museum there is an archaeological garden in which, among other exhibits, there are reconstructions of an Old Stone Age hut, a New Stone Age house and a dolmen; and the methods of working flint, carving bone, making primitive pottery and cave painting are demonstrated.

The **Aven de Marzal** is not quite as vast as Orgnac but is in many ways equally varied and impressive. Its different caves are 130m below ground level and are called the Hall of the Tomb, the Hall of the Dog, the Hall of the Pine Cone, the Hall of Columns, and the Hall of Diamonds. This last one scintillates with thousands of crystals in different colours, and is said by some to resemble a subterranean chapel with altar and candelabra.

The Aven de Marzal lies just north of the Gorges de l'Ardèche and can be reached from Vallon-Pont-d'Arc by the D4 to St Remèze and then the D201. It used to be called the Trou de la Barthe but its name changed in the early 19th century after a peasant of St Remèze named Boulle had murdered a forest guard who was called Marzal. Not knowing what to do with the body, he eventually threw it, together with the body of Marzal's dog, into the Trou de la Barthe. But as always it is in towns that nobody sees anything; in the remote country there always seems to be somebody watching,

and Boulle had been spotted. He was arrested by the gendarmes, and Marzal's body was found. The crime took place in 1812 and from that time on the locals began to refer to the place as the Grotte de Marzal.

This pothole was not properly explored until 1892, when the great speleologist E.-A. Martel investigated it. But later the entry became blocked, then overgrown, and finally forgotten. It was rediscovered in 1949, after a long search, by Pierre Ageron, and was soon afterwards opened to the public. The Hall of the Dog gets its name not from a stalagmite that looks like a dog, but from the skeleton of Marzal's dog found there.

There is an extra interest for cavers at Marzal, a small museum of speleology based on collections formed by Pierre Ageron, with clothing and equipment used at different times over the past hundred years by the most famous speleologists, from Martel to Norbert Casteret.

There is also something at Marzal which will appeal to children, a 'prehistoric zoo'. This consists of life-size reproductions of prehistoric animals of several different eras. They are cleverly disposed among the trees and bushes beside a shady path some hundreds of metres long. They include stegosaurus, tyrranosaurus and mammoth, and some of them are very convincing.

Some people do not like caves, but for those visitors who find them interesting, Orgnac and Marzal are good value. Even in summer the temperature in these cave systems does not exceed 14°C so remember to take a pullover or something warm to wear.

Among other underground wonders of Ardèche are the Aven de la

Forestière, not far from the Aven d'Orgnac, the Grotte de la Madeleine, reached through an opening in the cliff on the east side of the Gorges de l'Ardèche, and the Grottes de St Marcel. The Aven de la Forestière is easy of access, but rather less impressive than Orgnac. It has a specialist interest, however: a number of aquariums showing about 200 species of insects and fish which live in caves. The Grotte de la Madeleine is easily reached by a path from the D290. The Grottes de St Marcel, also reached from the D290, and not far from the southern end of the gorge, are remarkable for their great size and variety, and have only recently been equipped and opened to the general public.

Les Vans

Another off-the beaten-track excursion is to the town of **Les Vans** and some of the villages in its locality. Though there are no major sites on this tour, it is full of interest for the wildness and beauty of its scenery and the remoteness of the timeless villages, which in many respects seem not to belong to the 20th century at all.

Take the D104 from Aubenas to Lablachère and there fork right on to the D104a to Les Vans, about 36km in all. This town has a nicely restored old quarter, and a market place with an ancient fountain. Here you are at the edge of the Cévennes mountains, and for a number of years a local association has been encouraging peasants of the Cévennes to produce handmade articles of various kinds. A shop in the market place sells their work, which varies from wooden

carvings to knitwear and leather items, and it is a good place to buy souvenirs.

The village of Chambonas, just north of Les Vans, and on the river Chassezac, is approached across an unusual old bridge with triangular cut-waters, and has a four-towered château set in a formal French park and a 12th-century church. From Chambonas the D250 to Payzac and to St Jean-Porcherasse and then back to Chambonas via St Pierre-le-Déchausselat takes you through isolated old hamlets, as small as their names are big, and with only the breeze and the empty hills for company.

Just to the east of Les Vans via the D901 and then the D252 is the **Bois de Païolive**. This is an eerie and beautiful landscape, a chaos of weirdly shaped eroded limestone rocks, some like ruined houses or churches, some like the pillars of ancient temples, some like animals, all entangled in a forest of oak and chestnut. The D252 leads to a large clearing in the middle, where it is possible, especially on either side of the high season, to park the car and picnic in sylvan surroundings, and afterwards explore the wood for strange rock formations and find the belvedere overlooking the Chassezac.

This stretch of country is so mysterious and haunting that all sorts of legends have grown up about it. The local people believe that the souls of those who have died a violent death wander among the leafy shadows, as well as those of people who were unhappy in marriage and who come here looking for kindred souls with whom they might have been happy in life.

For visitors who want to stay and explore the area around Les Vans there is a pleasant hotel about 3km outside the town on the D104a, the Château le Scipionet, a top-grade Logis de France.

Just a couple of kilometres west of Les Vans by the D408 is Naves, a village which is still medieval in aspect and has an attractively sited Romanesque church. But the star of all these ancient and isolated villages, and the one that should not be missed, whether you stay or not, is **Thines**. Approached by a road beside a torrent which winds through a ravine, this perched village is a jumble of old houses in tangled narrow streets, with one of the best of the many superb Romanesque churches in this part of France. The church of Thines is approached up a wide, shallow stone staircase, incredibly old, and with wild rock plants growing between the stones. The building itself is remarkable, in this rugged and out of the way spot, for the quality and finesse of the carved stone decoration of the cornices, friezes and arcades in the upper part of the church, particularly those of the chevet. Inside it is one of those harmonious and serene old churches that make all but the most convinced atheists begin to wonder.

Thines is an altogether delightful village, and like Les Vans, it is a good place to buy examples of local craftsmanship as souvenirs.

In summer there is as much sun in Ardèche as there is on the Mediterranean coasts, but in the open spaces of these quiet, airy, lonely hills and valleys you are as far as it's possible to be in southern Europe from the world of the typical package tour.

Hotels & Restaurants

Prices: A = Very Expensive, B = Expensive, C = Moderately Expensive,
D = Average, E = Cheap.

AUBENAS (07200 Ardèche): **Panoramic Escrinet**, Col de l'Escrinet (75 87 10 11),
8km from Privas on the N104 towards Aubenas. Splendid situation at the top of
the pass. Garden, terrace, swimming pool, peaceful. Very good restaurant. Rooms
D. Meals C–D.

CRUAS (07350 Ardèche): **Le Chrystel** (75 51 43 10). Charming old-style bistrot
restaurant, but nothing outdated about the first-class and original cuisine. Meals
C–D.

LAMASTRE (07270 Ardèche): **Le Midi-Barrateiro** (75 06 41 50). A good restaurant
which is always improving. M. Perrier is a chef of talent and delivers very high
standards at fairly high prices for the deep countryside. A restaurant first but also
a sound family hotel in the traditional French manner. Rooms C–E. Meals C.

LARGENTIÈRE (07110 Ardèche): **Le Tanargue**, Valgorge (75 88 98 98). Modern
Logis de France in a remote and glorious country setting, with views over the
Cévennes. First-class food in attractive dining room or on terrace. Rooms D–E.
Meals D.

TOURNON (07300 Ardèche): **Château Hôtel de Paris**, 12 quai Marc Séguin
(75 08 60 22). Twin establishment, Logis de France. Restaurant with terrace overlooking the Rhône. Rooms D. Meals C–D.

VALS-LES-BAINS (07600 Ardèche): **St Jean** (75 37 42 50). Logis de France with a
better-than-average restaurant. Rooms D–E. Meals D–E.
La Truite Enchantée, pont de Labeaume, 07380 Lalevade de l'Ardèche (75 38 05 02),
4km west of Vals-les-Bains. The little (7 rooms) country inn par excellence. Simple,
neat, clean. Good restaurant, full board at less than the price of one meal in
many places. Rooms E. Meals E.
Chez Mireille (75 37 49 06). Small but professional restaurant. High standards at
modest prices. Meals D–E.

LES VANS (07140 Ardèche): **Château le Scipionnet** (75 37 23 84). Comfortable 19th-
century château in 25-acre park with good swimming pool. Room C. Meals C.

Châteaux, Sites etc: opening times

Note: am/pm means closed for lunch (normally for two hours).

TOURNON: **Château de Tournon**, am/pm from 1 June to 31 Aug, pm at other
times. Closed Wed and from 31 Oct to 1 April.

Vivarais Railway from Tournon to Lamastre. Departure from Tournon at 10.00. Every day in July and Aug. Tues–Sun from mid-May to 1 July and first fortnight of Sept. Return to Tournon at 18.00.

VOGÜÉ: Château de Vogüé, 15.00–18.00 July and Aug only. Sun only from Easter to July and in Sept.

LA MAS DE LA VIGNASSE: Alphonse Daudet's mill, am/pm from 1 May to 30 Sept, closed Tues.

UNDERGROUND ARDÈCHE: Aven d'Orgnac, am/pm from 1 March to 15 Nov. Visit one hour.
Aven de Marzal, open all day 16 April to 30 Sept. At 11.00, 15.30 and 17.00 from 1 March to 30 Nov, at weekends and holidays only. (*Note:* There are more than 700 steps in each of these caves.)

Leisure

FISHING There are numerous lakes and rivers for trout fishing, as well as coarse fishing, in Ardèche. Details from: Fédération Départementale des Associations Agrées de Pêche et de Pisciculture de L'Ardèche, 12 bld de la République, 07100 Annonay, Ardèche, or from the nearest Office de Tourisme or Syndicat d'Initiative.

CYCLING Ardèche is well organised for cycle tours; bicycles and cross-country bikes can be hired in many centres. Simple overnight accommodation with showers and loos can be arranged.

CANOE/KAYAK Rivers for all degrees of skill from beginners to the most expert. Information from: Fédération Française de Canoe-Kayak, 17 route de Vienne, 69007 Lyon.

WALKING Ardèche is wonderful country for walking tours with hundreds of kilometres of maintained footpaths. Information from: Comité Départementale de la Randonnée Pédestre, M. Jean Rouvière, 25 Allée de la Guingette, 07200 Aubenas, Ardèche.

HORSE-RIDING Ardèche is criss-crossed with pony-trekking circuits, and has two dozen riding centres. Riders' accommodation accepting only those on horseback is available. Information from: Comité Départementale du Tourisme Equestre, M. Massenet, le Pont-Sicard 07210 Chomérac.

Additional information can be obtained from the nearest Office de Tourisme, or from Direction Départementale de la Jeunesse et des Sports, 3 rue de Vanel, BP 625, 07006 Privas.

Tourist Information Offices

PRIVAS, 3 rue Elie Reynier (75 64 33 35).

Scale

30km

20

10

0

—N—

BRIANÇON

N91

Col du Galibier

Col du Lautaret

D902

La Grave

Alpine Garden

La Meije

La Tête de la Maye

La Bérarde

Le Rateau

Gorges de l'Infernet

Oratoire du Chazelet

Combe de Malaval

R Vénéon

L'Alpe d'Huez

Chambon

Les Ougiers

Massif des Ecrins

D211

Le Clapie

D530

St Christophe-en-Oisans

Lac Lauvitel

N91

Le Bourg d'Oisans

Gorges de la Romanche

Chaîne de Belledonne

Le Touvet

N90

Chartreuse de la

Massif

D512

Couvent de la Grande Chartreuse

St Pierre-de-Chartreuse

La Correrie

D520

Charmant Som

Bergeries

Col de Porte

D512

R Isère

R Romanche

GRENOBLE

St Martin-d'Hères

Vizille

Gorges de la Romanche

D5

N85

St Laurent-du-Pont

Belvédère des Sangles

Bois de Valombre

Voiron

N75

Sassenage

N85

R Drac

N532

Montagne de Lans

Villard-de-Lans

Parc Régional de Vercors

D531

Choranche Caves

Gorges de la Bourne

R Bourne

D103

Les Grands Goulêts

D518

Combe de Laval

D76

Pont-en-Royans

St Nazaire-en-Royans

La Machine

Vassieux-en-Venors

La Côte-St André

N85

98

7
Isère

The Autoroute du Soleil and the N7 down the east bank of the Rhône are roads best avoided during the summer holiday season, as they offer little but petrol fumes and a close view of the backs of container lorries. Vienne, which we left to cross to the west bank and the less crowded N86, is tucked away in a corner of the department of Isère, another area of magnificent scenery. Exploring it takes the visitor away from the Rhône Valley but for those who love mountains it is well worthwhile. The best base is in or near Grenoble, the heart of Isère, easily reached from Vienne by the D502, then the D518, D73, N85 and N75.

Grenoble, the prefecture of Isère, and the commercial and administrative capital of the French Alps, is a modern city known throughout France for its animation and the beauty of its setting. It lies in a plain at the junction of the rivers Isère and Drac, and is said to be the flattest city in France. But it is ringed on all sides by mountains, and because of its flatness there is hardly a street in Grenoble that does not have a view of mountains in at least one direction, and hardly a Grenoblois who does not have at least one window from which to look at the mountains in the changing light of the day, and

see the snow line alter as the seasons change.

There was a Celtic settlement here 2,000 years ago. When the Romans arrived, they fortified it with an encircling wall with several round towers, and built the first bridge across the Isère. But it was never an important Roman town, and it remained a small place throughout the Middle Ages. In 1219 a violent flood of the two rivers carried away the bridge, and it was many years before the town was entirely rebuilt.

Grenoble is also the capital of the region called the Dauphiné, which today consists of the departments of Isère, Drôme, and Hautes Alpes. The name is said to have originated in the 12th century, when the English wife of the lord of the region called her son Dolphin, which became translated into Dauphin in French. From this the lord became known as the Dauphin, and the area as the Dauphiné. In the early part of the 14th century the Dauphin was Humbert II, a young man of prodigal generosity towards the Church and all branches of the arts (he founded the University of Grenoble). Then, at great expense, he equipped a private army and joined a Crusade to the Holy Land. When he returned he found that both his wife

Maison du Tourisme Dauphiné/Grenoble

Looking down at the city of Grenoble

and his only son had died, and that his state was bankrupt. He sold it to the King of France, Philippe VI, in 1349, and retired to a Dominican monastery, where he died soon after. Part of the agreement had been that the Dauphiné would always revert to the eldest son of the royal family, who from that time was always known as the Dauphin of France.

Grenoble first became important in the 16th century when François de Bonne, Duc de Lesguidières, a brilliant soldier and administrator, commanded the Protestants of the Dauphiné during the religious wars. Henri IV later made him lieutenant general of the region to defend it against the ambitious dukes of Savoy.

Towards the end of the 19th century a Grenoble engineer named Aristide Berges installed a turbine to provide power for his paper mill at Lancey, just outside Grenoble. This was the first use of water power to provide electricity. Others followed suit and Grenoble steadily grew as an industrial town. It received a further boost when the city was host to the Winter Olympics in 1968, and, adding tourism to its commerical and administrative activities, it has developed rapidly since then.

The mountain ring around Grenoble is formed by the Massif de la Chartreuse in the north, and the wall of the high plateau of Vercors to the west. To the east is the wild Belledonne

The Musée Dauphinois is housed in one of Grenoble's more interesting old buildings

range, not crossed by any road, which formed the old border with Savoy. It is the first step towards the great Massif de la Vanoise. To the south of Grenoble is the valley of the Drac, flanked on the west by the Lans mountains, and on the east by the southern continuation of the Chaîne de Belledonne range, which sweeps on to the Massif des Ecrins, the largest national park in France.

All these areas, within easy reach of Grenoble, have destinations of remarkable beauty and interest for the summer visitor, as well as for winter sports enthusiasts. But Grenoble itself is more a tourist centre than a tourist destination. It is a good base, with a great variety of hotels and restaurants. Its animation is due to the large numbers of young people attached to its important university, and to its flourishing commerce which has attracted a congenial mix of people from all parts of France. There are a number of interesting things to see in the city itself. Probably the first thing for the visitor to do is to make the trip

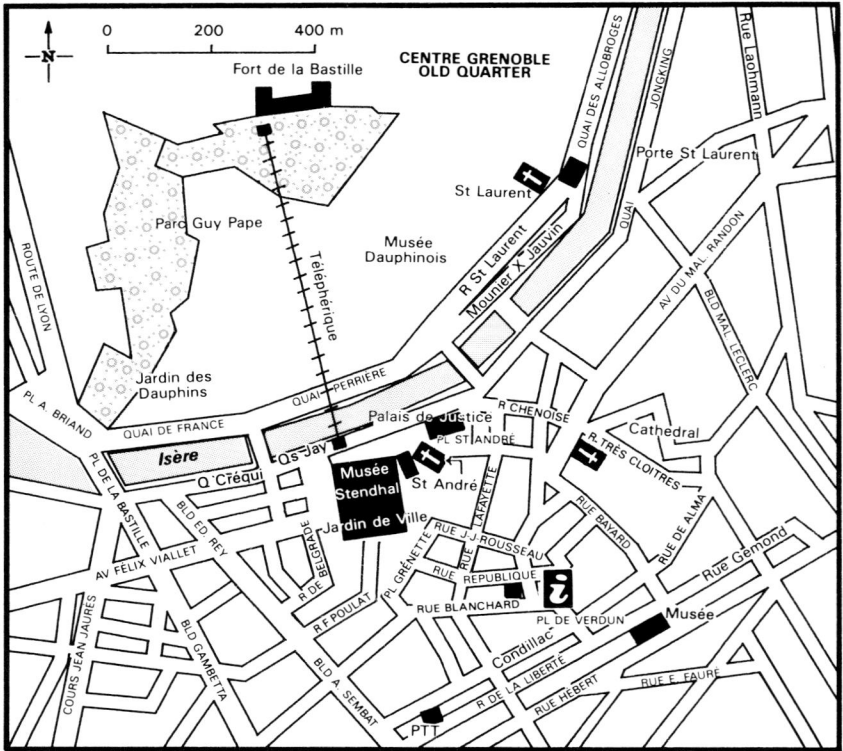

up to the Fort de la Bastille, on a height on the northern limit of the city, with splendid views over Grenoble itself and the junction of the two rivers, and of the mountains all around. Orientation tables make it easy to pick out the important mountains and chief points of interest. The fort can be reached by a cable car with unusual spherical, bubble-car cabins, which climb the 280m in little trains of five. It can also be reached by car, but if you go by cable car, you can have an interesting walk down by winding paths and stone staircases through pleasant gardens. There is a

good restaurant and bar at the top with a spacious terrace.

Grenoble has an attractive old quarter around the place St André, the church of St André, the Jardin de la Ville, and the place Grenette. The place St André is paved, and in the centre stands the statue of Bayard, the most famous of all French knights, the *chevalier sans peur et sans reproche*. He came from Pontcharra, north of Grenoble, and his castle,

In Grenoble you can take the téléferique up to the Fort de la Bastille

much restored and now privately owned, still stands. His tomb is in the church of St André. The Palais de Justice, the most impressive of the old buildings left in Grenoble, shares the place St André with the church and café terraces. This elegant building is partly Flamboyant Gothic and partly Renaissance in style.

In the nearby Jardin de la Ville, in part of the former town hall, there is a museum devoted to the writer Stendhal, who was born in Grenoble in 1783, son of a lawyer. In the actual house where he was born, No. 20 rue Jean Jacques Rousseau, close by, there is a museum concerning, not Stendhal, but the Second World War, with particular reference to the Resistance in the heights of Vercors and the Nazi concentration camps. The pedestrianised place Grenette is a favourite meeting place for the people of Grenoble, a nice mixture of shops and café terraces, and always animated.

Art lovers will enjoy a visit to the Museum of Painting and Sculpture in the place de Verdun which, in addition to a whole floor of old masters, has the finest collection in France, outside Paris, of modern and contemporary painting and sculpture.

The old quarter continues on the other side of the river beneath the slopes of the Fort de la Bastille, where the charming rue St Laurent leads to one of the old gates of the city, the Porte St Laurent, built in the early 17th century by Lesdiguières, and to the church of St Laurent. The church itself is of no special interest, but is built over a chapel of the 6th and 7th centuries dedicated to St Oyand, which now forms the crypt of the church. This ancient chapel, one of the three oldest in France, was built on the site of a Gallo-Roman burial place and is noteworthy for its fine marble pillars and carved capitals. Apart from its old quarter, Grenoble cannot be said to be architecturally interesting or beautiful, and some of its modern buildings are conspicuously aggressive, but if there are ugly factories and graceless tower blocks here and there, and other evidence of too rapid and expedient development, all this is dwarfed by the wonderful surroundings. The vision of the setting sun turning the heights of the Belledonne range rose, and then purple; on crystal clear nights the lights dotted about the mountainsides easily mistaken for stars; in winter the sparkling white of the sunlit peaks; all these are small benedictions that can make even the busiest people in the city pause in their stride. The inhabitants of Grenoble, more than those in most cities, are fortunate in being so close to nature, and in knowing that they can get away so easily to their own favourite spot in the wilderness that surrounds their civilisation.

Grenoble is a base from which an inquisitive visitor can set out in any direction and find something well worth his time. But there are several excursions, both short and long, which are of special interest. Only 15km to the south of Grenoble, via the N85 or the D5 (a far more attractive route) is **Vizille**, a mainly industrial town, but one which does have an historic château, one of the finest and most interesting of the early 17th century. It was built for Lesdiguières between 1600 and 1620 as a fortress, and so has a rather severe façade overlooking the river Romanche. When his son-in-law, the Marshal de Crequi, inherited the property, he added a splendid staircase

The early 17th-century Château de Vizille, south of Grenoble

in double zig-zag with balconies on the side of the château facing the park. He also had an ornamental lake dug and stocked it with hundreds of trout. The park side of the château, with one round tower with a conical roof and one square tower with a four-sided dome and cupola, the elegant staircase, and the graceful swans on the lake, is altogether less rugged than that seen from the banks of the Romanche.

The interior of the château was badly damaged by fire in the 19th century, but it was restored and refurnished and became an official summer home for French presidents until 1972, when President de Gaulle opened it to the public. There is plenty to see inside in the way of period furniture, tapestries, and paintings, as well as a recently established museum of the French Revolution.

A little further along the N85 from Vizille is the miniature railway of La Mure (see box).

Another good short excursion takes you 27km to the north of Grenoble along the N90, through the valley of the Isère to **Le Touvet**. Here, there is a château of quite a different kind — small, charming, a family home, never a fortress. It was originally just a watch tower but was steadily enlarged and altered throughout the Middle Ages. It eventually became the property of

A Ticket to Ride

The La Mure railway is one of the most spectacular in the world, and certainly offers the most dramatic ride in the Alps. This line was opened in 1888 to carry passengers and coal the 30km between St Georges de Commiers and La Mure. In 1903 it became the world's first high-tension electric railway. The carriages and engines used today are all beautifully maintained museum pieces – passenger coaches from 1915 to 1932, self-propelled coaches from 1915 to 1927, and locomotives from 1932. The line has 133 bends, 18 tunnels, and twelve viaducts, passes through gorges and beside lakes, and gives views of the mountains, the cliffs of Vercors, and the snow-covered heights of Oisans, not visible from any road.

The trains run regularly every day from 1 June to 23 September, and at week-ends and on public holidays at other times of the year, and by special arrangement for groups, when other passengers may also be taken. The station at St Georges de Commiers is about 20km from Grenoble by the N85 to Champ sur Drac, and the D529.

Full details of services from: Chemin de Fer de la Mure, 38450 St Georges de Commiers, or Maison du Tourisme, 14 rue de la République, 38000 Grenoble.

the family of Monteynard de Marcieu who still have it today. Between 1753 and 1777 Count Pierre de Marcieu made the alterations which gave the château its most unusual and attractive feature, a magnificent galleried staircase in stone with ornamental wrought iron balustrades. One of the earlier owners of the château, Gigues Guifrey, was François I's ambassador at the English court of Henry VIII, and among a number of interesting old documents exhibited in the gallery are letters signed by Henry VIII and François I. Pierre de Marcieu also had the rooms furnished with fine pieces made to order by local cabinet makers. The grounds were transformed by the creation of a splendid water staircase descending in a series of ponds and cascades, fed by streams from the Massif de la Grande Chartreuse,

through formal French gardens and avenues of trees.

A slightly longer trip from Grenoble, about 40km each way, which may appeal to music lovers, is to **La Côte-St André**. This town, situated midway between Grenoble and Vienne, on the D73, is built on the side of a hill overlooking a sunny plain to the south. It was the birthplace of the composer Hector Berlioz. The town still has its 16th-century wooden market hall, a *tour de force* of great roof beams and wooden pillars, which is the setting in September every year of an international music festival in honour of Berlioz. He was born in 1803, the son of a prosperous local doctor, at 89 rue de la République, and lived there until he was 17. The house was restored in 1969 and is now a museum with many souvenirs of the composer, including his first musical instruments – a flute, a clarinet, and a guitar, which he is said to have smashed in anger.

Near the 16th-century market hall there are some old houses with wooden balconies, and the town has a château, rebuilt in the 17th century and restored since, and an old church, dating from the 12th–15th centuries. This old church has an unusual tower, built in pebbles and brick with corners in whitish stone, giving it an unusual coloration in addition to an attractive shape. It was often painted by the Dutch artist Jongkind, who spent the last 14 years of his life at La Côte-St André. At his best Jongkind was one of the great landscape painters of the 19th century, and a precursor of Impressionism, but he was also in later life an alcoholic who eventually drank himself into insanity, and on the way often turned out facile pictures, unworthy of his talent, for quick commercial returns. He is buried in the cemetery at La Côte-St André.

The drive to the **Massif de la Grand Chartreuse** from Grenoble along the D512 is a scenic one, with the added interest of seeing the headquarters of the Carthusian Order and the place where probably the world's best-known liqueur, and according to some connoisseurs the finest, originated. The domain of La Grande Chartreuse and the monastery itself are not open to the public, but nearby at La Correrie there is a Carthusian museum full of things relating to the Carthusians, which offers an audio-visual presentation of the history and development of the order over the centuries, and explains the day to day life of a Carthusian monk. Unlike most religious orders, the rules of the Carthusians have never been changed since the order was founded in the 11th century. Each monk lives in his own cell, which gives on to a cloister. It is a solitary life; only one meal a week is taken in common in the refectory. Other meals are left at the cell door.

Once a week the monks walk in the woods that surround the monastery, sometimes collecting the herbs necessary for the making of the famous liqueur. The rest of their time is taken up in attending religious services several times a day, intellectual pursuits and manual labour.

To reach the Massif take the D512 out of Grenoble on the eastern side of the Fort de la Bastille. The road at once begins to twist and climb, often steeply, until it reaches the Col de Porte, at almost 1,200m. Here a narrow road, the D57d, leads off briefly to the left towards the height called Charmant Som. The road comes to an end after about 4km at a place called Les Bergeries, where the car can be left, and a half-hour walk brings you to the highest point, from which there is a view of the buildings of La Grande Chartreuse, as well as an extremely varied and interesting panorama all around.

Return to the Col de Porte and continue on the D512 towards St Pierre-de-Chartreuse, downhill. Those interested in church interiors may like to turn off temporarily to the right on the D579 which leads quickly to the very unusual church of St Hugues, 3km away. The interior has been entirely decorated in contemporary style between the years 1953 and 1986 by one artist, Jean Marie Piot Arcabas. All the painting, using a lot of red and gold, the sculpture, and the stained glass and sacred objects are his work.

Water of Life

No liqueur is a mere drink. As all advertising men are aware, they are 'magic potions' with unknown and mysterious ingredients mixed in secrecy by alchemists sworn to silence. But the finest of them all, Chartreuse, is an instance of fact is stranger than any marketing fiction. The chronological history of this liqueur speaks for itself:

16th century: An unknown genius concocted a remarkable liqueur. When and where is not known, and it was not put on sale.

17th century: The Marshal d'Estrées (brother of the notorious and glamorous Gabrielle, mistress of King Henri IV) acquired the recipe early in the century. Perhaps thinking that 130 herbs infused in cognac would do little but spoil the brandy, he gave the formula and the long list of ingredients to the Carthusian monks in Paris in 1605.

18th century: The Carthusians of Paris, having realised after 130 years that almost none of the required herbs were readily obtainable in the heart of Paris, gave the recipe in 1737 to the Prior General at the Grande Chartreuse in the wilds of Isère.

18th century–later: Not only was the Grande Chartreuse entirely surrounded by herbs waiting to be infused in brandy, it also had a monk who was a superb chemist. This Brother Jerome experimented for years and at last added three more refinements bringing the liqueur near to perfection. Overcome with the excitement of success he died in his laboratory, just having time to gasp out the improved formula before, as they say in French, 'rendering his last sigh', which may well have been one of regret.

From St Hugues the road carries on back to the D512, which it rejoins before the village of St Pierre-de-Chartreuse, where it bears left and becomes the D520. After about 2km towards St Laurent-du-Pont, a short road on the left leads to a point where you can leave the car and follow a signposted path through the Bois de Vallombre towards the Belvédère des Sangles. The walk to the belvedere and back takes about 2½ hours, but you do not have to go all the way to have a closer view of the monastery of the Grande Chartreuse, because the footpath quite soon comes to the clearing of Valombre, from which the monastery buildings can be seen. Return to the D520 and continue towards St Laurent-du-Pont. Almost at once a narrow (one-way) road on the right leads to La Correrie and the Carthusian museum.

The D520 continues through a luxuriantly wooded gorge called Guiers Mort, with in places vertical limestone cliffs above the forested slopes. If you have walked through the pure mountain air to any of the viewpoints you are certain to have a keen appetite and, if the time is ripe, lunch can be taken in St Pierre-de-Chartreuse or in

1764: Brother Antoine at the Grande Chartreuse made the liqueur commercially in two kinds, one for table use, one medicinal.

Mid-18th century–end: French Revolution. The monks were evicted from the Grande Chartreuse. One monk, Brother Sebastian, was given the secret. He was imprisoned in Bordeaux and sentenced to be transported to Guyana and died on board ship. The secret was lost? No. In prison he had confided it to a friend.

1817: The monks and the recipe returned to the Grande Chartreuse. Somehow a chemist acquired the original manuscript, now more than two hundred years old, and tried to sell it to the Government. They showed no interest in the dirty old papers.

1835: The recipe returned to the Grande Chartreuse, and successful production was at last established. A lay clerk tried to make his fortune by stealing the recipe. He was in such a hurry to pack and get away that he left it on his bed.

1903: The French government expelled the Carthusians from France. They went to Spain and continued to make Chartreuse. In France, the Government took over production, and continued for 25 years, but their version was hopelessly inferior.

1940: The monks returned to the Grand Chartreuse, and made both the green and the yellow versions there. Success led to success, and the liqueur is now produced at a large commercial distillery in Voiron. Many people work there, but the secret remains with the monks. There are still only two copies of the recipe, one with the Prior General and one in a bank safe deposit.

St Laurent-du-Pont. Both these little villages are popular centres for walking holidays in the Massif de la Chartreuse which, although it has very few roads, is criss-crossed by a number of sign-posted footpaths, and both centres are equipped with hotels and restaurants. There are ten in St Pierre-de-Chartreuse and two in St Laurent-du-Pont. The day's outing can conclude by continuing on the D520 to Voiron, a busy and not very interesting commercial town, except that it is here that the famous Chartreuse liqueurs are produced today, under the supervision of monks who spend three months at

a time there. The modern cellars are open to the public, and there are exhibitions and video films made by the brothers themselves illustrating each stage of the manufacture. It is a fascinating visit, and if you have had lunch, a good digestif in itself.

Apart from these more or less civilised excursions Grenoble offers the touring motorist a chance to see something on a bigger and more rugged scale. The city is a gateway to Europe's greatest mountain range, the harsh, majestic and beautiful chain of the Alps, which begins east of Grenoble. Only one main road exists in this direction, the N91 from Grenoble to Briançon, a distance of 108km. It is enough to follow it the 80km to the Col du Lautaret, and then turn off to the north the 7km to the Col du Galibier, to find yourself driving through a world of mountain peaks where nothing diminishes the grand solitude.

The N91 begins by running south to Vizille before turning east through the disappointingly unlovely and industrialised valley of the Romanche. But it is not long before things improve and the remaining 60km to the Col du Lautaret are consistently picturesque or spectacular. The road passes through one of the wildest and loneliest parts of France where, in some areas, there are more mountain peaks than there are inhabitants. Despite its emptiness it is an old road, first constructed by the Romans in the first century BC, from Briançon to Grenoble, then called Brigantia and Cularo, and for hundreds of years, almost its only use was for occasional military purposes. Even in the 19th century it was reckoned that on average only one person per week passed the Col du Lautaret. It is an incredibly wild region, where the winter is iron hard, and the summer storms ferociously severe, though spring and summer also see long spells of crystal clear sunny weather. The land is rocky and infertile, but is one of the richest in the world in the variety of minerals which can be found there – gold, silver, iron, lead, copper, cobalt, nickel, talc and anthracite, but all in small quantities. One mineralogist called it the 'Eldorado of samples'.

Around the village of St Christophe-en-Oisans, just over 100 permanent inhabitants live in the (geographically) second largest commune in France, 24,287ha (although the village itself is tiny and in winter has as few as eight inhabitants). But this is well away from the N91, which passes through **Le Bourg d'Oisans**, the only little town on the road, a market place and commercial centre for a vast mountain region, and now a tourist centre. From Le Bourg d'Oisans the road becomes more picturesque, climbing after a few kilometres up the steep Rampe des Commères, which might be freely translated as Chatterbox Hill. The sharp incline is no bother to modern cars, but was much feared in the days of stage coaches, when passengers were obliged to get down and walk as the horses struggled up the slope, a situation which caused a good deal of excitement, complaint and chatter. Then the road follows the rugged Gorge d'Infernet, and then the Barrage du Chambon, built across a narrow part of the valley of the Romanche, and holding back a large artificial lake which swallowed up three of the local hamlets as the waters rose to fill it.

Beyond the Barrage du Chambon and La Grave, the next village, the N91 passes through the long defile of the Combe de Malaval, whose rocky sides are varied only by an occasional impressive waterfall and belts of larch woods.

In recent years **La Grave** has become a popular winter sports resort but for many years prior to that it was, like Chamonix and Zermatt, a climbing centre known to serious mountaineers the world over. It still has only a few hundred permanent inhabitants, but has several hotels and restaurants, and is a convenient stop for lunch. It also offers a couple of good mini-excursions. The cable car which serves the ski slopes also operates during July and August, and takes you up 3,200m to the Col des Ruillans on the north-west slope of Mont Rateau. From the col there are unforgettable views of the triple-peaked La Meije, one of the loveliest of all the alpine mountains, and the last of all the French Alps to be climbed. This half-hour trip can be made either before or after lunch.

On the northern side of the N91, the D33a leads to the viewpoint called L'Oratoire du Chazelet from which there are more distant views of La Meije and mountains further to the south in the Parc National des Ecrins.

From La Grave the N91 climbs for a further 11km to the Col du Lautaret. It is worth stopping here, not only for the views but also to see the Alpine Garden, founded nearly a hundred years ago by the University of Grenoble. The site, covering more than 2ha, has alpine and medicinal plants collected from mountain ranges in many different parts of the world, arranged according to their geographical origin. The garden is best seen in July and August, when it is in full flower. There is a beautiful view of the Massif de la Meije and its glaciers.

From the N91 at the Col du Lautaret the D902 turns off to the north, and in 7km climbs another 600m to the Col du Galibier, an historical frontier post between France and Savoy. In clear weather this is one of the best viewpoints in all Europe, with a stupendous panorama in all directions.

If the Oisans area seems wild and wonderful to the visitor, the country to the south, now the Parc National des Ecrins, the largest national park in France, is even more impressive. This park was established in 1973 after several years of planning during which the Government acquired land from various communes. It covers 100,000ha in which dogs, hunting, cars, caravans, camping and hotels are all banned, and is surrounded by another protected area of 177,000ha, in which tourist and craft activities are permitted, and in which there are several ski resorts.

Much of the park is the world as it was, untouched by man. The easiest approach from Le Bourg d'Oisans is to follow the N91 to Le Clapie and turn off on to the D530 which follows the valley of the Vénéon to the hamlet of La Bérarde. It is for much of the way a desperately exciting rather than a picturesque route, the valley often being shut in by mountain walls up to 1,500m high which, except for occasional glimpses, hide the mountain peaks. I have said it is the easiest approach from Le Bourg d'Oisans, but it is nevertheless a difficult and dangerous route, which will add something to any motorist's experience. It is well maintained but very narrow, a mixture of very steep climbs and twists and turns, with precipitous drops close at hand.

Walkers may want to go no further than Les Ougiers, where a road turns off to the south for 2½km to a point where the car can be left, and there is an attractive walk to the picturesque Lac Lauvitel. The walk, which takes about three hours there and back, is along a signposted footpath, with occasional notices referring to the

Overleaf: *Alpe d'Huez provides a striking example of the stunning mountain scenery around Grenoble*

flora and fauna and geology of the region, which are explained in more detail in books sold in information centres in the Parc National des Ecrins. Waterfalls, mountain torrents and views of the mountain peaks add variety to what is a pleasant walk.

But some motorists may wish to push on to **St Christophe-en-Oisans**. The name of this tiny village, is, like that of Chamonix, legendary in the world of international mountaineers. Some idea of its significance can be gathered by looking at the little cemetery, which occupies the only piece of flat land in the hamlet. Here are buried some of the great names among alpine guides, the Gaspards, the Turcs, the Rodiers, men of the village side by side with some of the pioneer climbers who came from outside and lost their young lives in challenging the icy heights. Some of the headstones are slabs taken from the mountains and carved in rough outlines of particular peaks, with small crosses cut into them to show where the climbers died. These simple graves, and a look around at the wilderness of mountains, say more about the spirit of man than a whole library of philosophical works.

But even at St Christophe, remote as it is, you are not actually in the park itself. It is another 11km to La Bérarde, which is one of the gateways to the **Parc des Ecrins**.

You do not need to be a mountaineer to make the ascent of the Tête de la Maye (2,519m) from La Bérarde, but you should be an experienced mountain walker. The climb up takes about 2½ hours, and from the top there are panoramic views. The descent takes about half as long.

An alternative, somewhat easier walk, is the two hours there and back

from La Bérarde to the Plan du Carrelet, which takes you into the park following the valley of the Vénéon. Properly maintained mountain chalets and dormitories exist at La Bérarde and throughout the park at sensible intervals, but no one who is not fit, experienced and correctly equipped – an ice axe is useful – should contemplate walking in these rugged mountains. There are more than 1,000km of maintained footpaths, including the GR54, the GR541 and the GR50. It is possible for serious walkers to make a ten-day tour of the park, about 180km, using the signposted footpaths and the chalets on or near them. Wildlife in the park includes more than 5,000 chamois, and there are more than 3,000 species of plants and flowers.

The other mountainous region which lies on the threshold of Grenoble is Vercors, to the south and west. It is an area of mountains and high plateaux, an area where rich green pastures alternate with great forests of beech and pine, of remote villages held in the time-trap of the past, of isolated farms, dramatic gorges and secret caves. It is a place where despite the wildness and the loneliness – there are fewer than two inhabitants to the square kilometre – there is, in addition to its beauty, rather more of interest and rather more in the way of amenities than in Isère's other mountain areas.

The **Parc Naturel Régional de Vercors** was created in 1970 and covers an area of 135,000ha. It was founded in order to protect the natural environment, but as with most other regional nature parks, also with the idea of developing local agriculture, small industries and crafts, and above all tourism, as it was already an important aspect of the local economy. The park's charter foresaw the further development of open-air activities in Vercors, including climbing, caving and rambling. Over 100km of signposted paths have been provided for walking, cycling, and horse-riding, and around Autrans and Villard-de-Lans, there are signposted routes for cross-country skiing. These resorts also have facilities for alpine skiing, and Villard-de-Lans has a toboggan run, while at St Nizier there are good ski-jumping facilities.

Vercors is the most southerly of the Alpine massifs, and although it has several winter-sports centres, the summers are warm, the alpine meadows are thick with flowers, and the winter resorts are also well equipped for the summer tourist. There are numerous excursions and activities for the holidaymaker.

Villard-de-Lans is one of the best bases. It is situated in an open valley surrounded by mountain and forest, and its pure air and sunny climate, and the number of excursions possible in the area, make it a popular summer destination. To reach it take the N532 out of Grenoble, turning left on to the D531 at Sassenage.

One excursion which gives a good idea of the combination of beauty and excitement which Vercors offers is from Villard-de-Lans to Pont-en-Royans via the D531 through the **Gorges de la Bourne**, returning via the Grands Goulets and the D103. The D531 soon enters a narrow gorge, where the road and the river dispute pride of place. When you see it reduced to a thickle at the end of the dry summer, it is difficult to imagine the ferocity of the torrent in spring after the melting of

the winter snow, but the gorge itself, with overhanging cliffs, is always impressive. In places the rich vegetation looks as if it must have been attached to the sheer cliff face with superglue.

This gorge is one of many in Vercors, a massif consisting almost entirely of limestone, which over thousands of years has been worn away by water. So there is another Vercors underground, with huge caves, subterranean rivers and lakes. This is a world known only to cavers, apart from a few of the more accessible caves which have been opened to the public. As you descend this gorge, it gradually widens, and the **Chorance caves**, the most spectacular of those open to the public, are just off the D531. A road about 2½km long leads to a parking place. The Grotte de Coufin was first discovered in 1875 and since then about 13km of underground galleries have been explored in the Chorance complex, but the visit is confined to an area of easy access near the entrance. In an underground chamber 16m high and 70m wide there are thousands of pure white needle-like stalactites up to 3m long, reflected in the water of a lake formed by the meeting of two underground streams. These formations together with those in an adjacent gallery that forms part of the tour, are believed to be unique in Europe. Those visitors inclined to believe that one cave is much like another will be surprised by this one, where clever lighting enhances the already unusual character.

Pont-en-Royans has some ancient houses perched on a cliff edge and apparently supported by great wooden beams set into the rock face above the river.

The D518 back to Villard-de-Lans
through the Grand Goulets is an
even more dramatic route. It follows
the valley of the Vernaison with perpendicular cliffs closing in to form a
sinister defile. The road, cut under
the cliffs or in tunnels through them,
has to be driven with caution, and
though it offers some fine views of
the Vernaison, it is not likely to be the
driver who sees them. But it is possible
to stop here and there, and as you
approach the Grands Goulets, it is a
good idea to park and walk ahead to
get an idea of the nature of the road.

From Pont-en-Royans the motorist
also has the opportunity of driving on
one of the most spectacular roads in
the whole of France. The distance is
less than 20km, but unforgettable. This
extraordinary road was built at the
end of the 19th century by the Ministry
of Waters and Forests, who wanted to
create an easier way to bring the
timber down from the huge forest of
Lente to the sawmills in the valleys.
They decided to cut a road like a step
in the 600m perpendicular cliffs of
Combe de Laval, a blind valley. The
road which starts at the Col de la
Machine has vertical cliffs on one side
and a vertical drop on the other, and
passes under stone arches and through
tunnels cut in the rock. There are
splendid views across to the wooded
slopes on the other side of the valley,
and of the Chome river 600m below
the road and the rolling countryside
of Royans.

An alternative base to Villard-de-
Lans, for those who find it more convenient to explore Vercors from the
south, is **Vassieux-en-Vercors**. During
the Second World War this was a key
base for the French Resistance who
built a landing strip meant for Allied

*The hair-raising corniche road at
Combe de Laval*

use, but on 21 July 1944 it was the
German troops who landed there. They
destroyed Vassieux and several other
villages, killing almost 1,000 Resistance
fighters and local inhabitants, and even
assassinated the wounded they found
in an improvised hospital in the Grotte
de la Luire and their two doctors.

Vassieux has since been completely
rebuilt. Two of the wartime gliders
remain, one in front of the church,
and one in front of a small museum
of the Resistance.

Excursions to the Gorges de la Bourne, the Grands Goulets, and Combe de Laval can equally well be made from Vassieux. About 3km to the south of the town there is a prehistoric toolmaker's workshop which specialised about 4,000 years ago in the making of stone knives and daggers which were exported to various parts of Europe. Demonstrations are given showing the way different tools were made, and there are also audio-visual explanations.

The plateau of Vercors in fact is shared by two departments; the north-eastern part is in Isère and the south-west in Drôme. Though slightly closer to Villard-de-Lans, Combe de Laval, and the Grand Goulets gorge are actually in the north-east corner of Drôme, as is Vassieux-en-Vercors.

Hotels & Restaurants

Prices: A = Very Expensive, B = Expensive, C = Moderately Expensive, D = Average, E = Cheap.

LA CÔTE-ST ANDRÉ (38260 Isère): **Hôtel de l'Europe**, 20 rue de la République (74 20 53 10). Typical Logis de France with good regional restaurant. Rooms and meals D–E.
Les Donnières, Mottier (74 54 42 06), 9km north-east of La Côte-St André, in the village of Mottier near the Mairie. Very good value traditional restaurant. Meals C–D.

LES DEUX ALPES: Chalet Mounier (76 80 56 90). Well-equipped modern mountain chalet hotel. Heated pool, tennis etc. Closed mid-Sept to mid-Dec, and 1 May to 20 June. Rooms and meals C–D.

LA GRAVE (05320 Hautes Alpes): **La Meijette** (76 79 90 34). A Logis de France with a sound restaurant. Rooms and meals D.

GRENOBLE (38000 Isère): **Mercure**, 1 av d'Innsbruck (76 09 54 27). Modern well-equipped hotel handy for Lyon-Grenoble autoroute. Swimming pool. Rooms C–D. Meals D.
Rive Droite, 20 quai de France (76 87 61 11). Good hotel in a modernised 19th-century building. Rooms and meals D.
Alpha, 34 av de Meylan, 38240 Meylan (76 90 63 09). Newish hotel with spacious rooms, 3km north-east of Grenoble by the Geneva road (N90). Swimming pool and terrace. Rooms C–D. Meals D.
A Ma Table, 92 cours Jean Jaurès (76 96 77 04). Small (booking advised) restaurant but reliable and original cuisine. Closed in Aug. Meals C.
L'Escale, 4 pl des Gordes (76 51 65 67). Modest restaurant in the old quarter of Grenoble. Good food and good service. Terrace. Closed Mon. Meals D–E.
Thibaud, 25 bld Agutte-Sembat, near Post Office (76 43 01 62). Small (booking advised) serious restaurant in the classical manner, with fresh market produce and regional recipes. One of the few in the city open every day all year. Meals C–D.

ST PIERRE-DE-CHARTREUSE: Auberge de l'Atre Fleuri, route de Col de Porte, 38380 St Laurent-du-Pont (76 88 60 21). Simple, charming, well-run with reliable restaurant. Rooms and meals E.

PONT-EN-ROYANS (38360 Isère): **Beau Rivage** (76 36 00 63). Straightforward Logis de France with better-than-average restaurant. Rooms and meals D–E.

LE TOUVET (38660 Isère): **Auberge St Vincent** (76 08 46 97). Nice little inn on the slopes of the Massif de la Grande Chartreuse. Rooms D. Meals C–D.

VILLARD-DE-LANS (38250 Isère): **Le Pré Fleuri**, av Albert Pietri (76 95 10 96). In a tranquil spot at the edge of the village. Modern chalet hotel. Closed Easter to Whitsun and 1 Oct to 20 Dec. Rooms D. Meals C–E.

Châteaux, Museums, Sites etc: opening times

Note: am/pm means closed for lunch (normally for two hours).

CHORANCHE: Grotte de Coufin, am/pm all year round.

COL DU LAUTARET: Alpine Garden, am/pm June–Sept.

LA CORRERIE: Carthusian Museum, am/pm April to Oct.

LA CÔTE-ST ANDRÉ: Berlioz Museum, am/pm from 1 March to 31 Dec, pm only in Feb, closed on Mon and in Jan.

GRENOBLE: Stendhal Museum, pm only, closed Mon and public holidays. **Museum of Painting and Sculpture**, am/pm all year, closed Tues.

LA MURE: Miniature Railway, service from May to Oct. Information on train times from Maison de Tourisme, Grenoble.

LE TOUVET: Château le Touvet, open from May to Oct, pm on Sat, Sun and public holidays.

VIZILLE: Château de Vizille, am/pm all year. Closed Tues and from mid-Dec to mid-Jan.

VOIRON: Chartreuse Cellars, am/pm daily from Easter to All Saints; rest of the year weekdays only.

Leisure

HORSE-RIDING There are several centres in the Grenoble area. Information from ARATE, 14 rue de la République, 38000 Grenoble.

CANOE-KAYAK Comité Départementale de Canoe-kayak, 163 av Ambroise-Croizat, 38400 St Martin d'Heres (south-east Grenoble).

HILL AND MOUNTAIN WALKING in national and regional parks: check at the Office de Tourisme, Grenoble or at local Syndicats d'Initiatives.

Tourist Information Offices

GRENOBLE – 14 rue République (76 54 34 36).

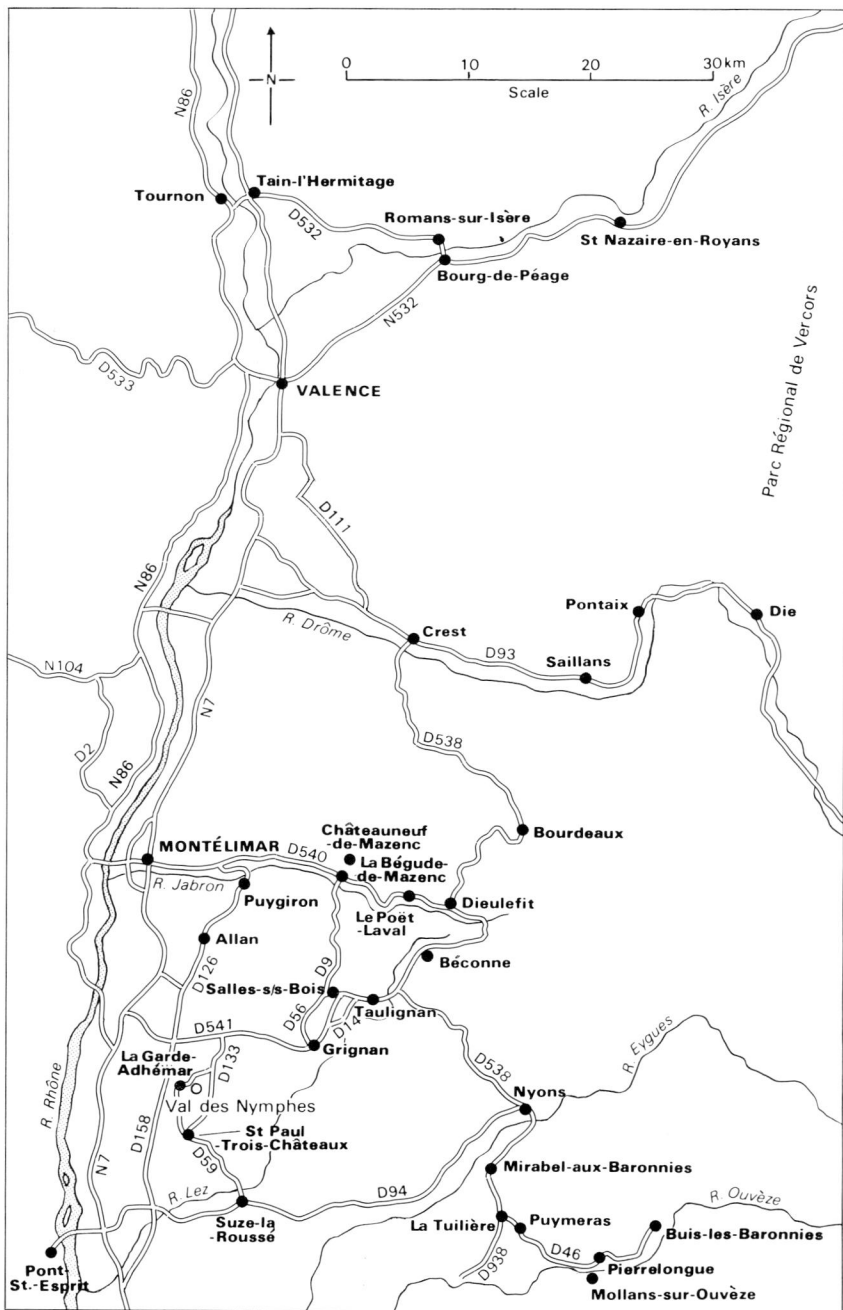

8
Drôme

Valence, the prefecture and commercial capital of the department of Drôme, is situated on a terrace on the east bank of the Rhône, looking across to the cliffs of Ardèche, capped by the ruins of the castle of Crussol. For the visitor from the north of France, its red-tiled houses and sunny streets, its markets full of the fruits of the south, make it the first town of the Rhône that seems to belong to the Midi. It is 100km south of Lyon, and 125 north of Avignon, and is the business centre of the mid-Rhône.

Though Valence was founded by the Romans, who called it Valentia Augusta, little remains of its Roman past. There is known to be a Roman theatre but it lies beneath the houses of the old quarter, near the church of St Jean. The town became a bishopric in the 4th century AD and was governed by its bishops throughout the Middle Ages. Later it was the capital of the Duchy of Valentinois, which at one time or another was owned by Cesare Borgia, Diane de Poitiers and Henri Grimaldi, Prince of Monaco.

The most interesting of its monuments is the St Apollinaire Cathedral, originally built in the 11th century, destroyed during the religious wars, and rebuilt at the beginning of the

17th century as a copy of the original. The impressive interior is in the Romanesque style as used in Auvergne, and it is one of the few cathedrals in the south-east with a deambulatory with radiating chapels. The tower is a 19th-century replacement of one burned down in 1838.

A short walk from the cathedral, at No. 57 Grande Rue, there is a Renaissance mansion called the Maison des Têtes, from the row of sculptured heads at first-floor level representing great thinkers and philosophers of antiquity. Nine of the original sixteen remain. The Italianate façade also includes life-size figures beneath the roof line. The building is a good example of the way in which the Renaissance spread from Italy through Europe. In 1515 Antoine de Dorne, a prosperous lawyer and professor at the University of Valence made a journey to Italy. On his return he determined to build a house in the new style which he had seen there. It was finished in 1532, the first Renaissance mansion in Valence, and evidence of the prosperity of the town in the early part of the 16th century.

In the municipal museum in the former bishop's palace next to the cathedral there is a large collection of 17th-century red chalk drawings

The Robin Hood of the Rhône

One of the factors which helped to create a revolutionary climate in 18th-century France was the chaos of excessive taxation. Among the goods most heavily taxed were salt, tobacco, silk and other exotic cloths from abroad, and jewellery. Taxes, and thus the price of goods, varied from town to town, from north to south, and from east to west. The taxes were collected with savage brutality and a total indifference to justice. On the night of 6 July 1753 a boatman on the Rhône was challenged by a tax collector. Before he had time to pull in to the bank he was shot dead. Nothing illegal was found in his boat, but the court took the view that the collector had been doing his duty and the man was acquitted.

In the face of this sort of treatment the smugglers organised themselves into armed bands. They had friends everywhere ready to help them against the hated excise men. Innkeepers and café owners bought their goods, regular soldiers smoked their tobacco, and the village priests would hide men and goods, even in the church itself.

The most famous of these smugglers was Louis Mandrin, who led a band of 120 men. He was described at the time as 'handsome, bold, intrepid, patient and ingenious'. His band would ride into a town and conduct their own market of contraband goods in broad daylight. By the time the authorities were alerted, Mandrin and his men were up and away, and always escaped their pursuers. When in a hurry Mandrin would hold the local dealers in salt or tobacco to ransom, telling them they had to pay his price for his goods or face the consequences. Mandrin was well known for his generosity to the poor and his gallantry to the ladies, and all this combined with his ability to make the tax men look ridiculous made him the stuff of legend in his short life. He soon developed the remarkable ability to be in two or more places at once. His friends 'betrayed' him to the authorities in one town, while he safely raided another miles away.

But eventually he was really betrayed, and captured. He was imprisoned in Valence, and sentenced to be broken on the wheel. He was executed on 6 May 1755. He was 30 years old, and one of 767 smugglers condemned in a period of 20 years. To his executioner, Mandrin said, 'Do your duty, my friend, as quickly as you can', and while his confessor fainted, Mandrin drank a glass of wine to give himself courage. After eight minutes of torture which he bore in silence, the Robin Hood of the Rhône was strangled, a favour granted at the request of the Bishop of Valence.

The sculptures on the façade of the renaissance Maison des Têtes in Valence represent ancient thinkers and philosophers (sanguines) by Hubert Robert. There are also some Gallo-Roman mosaics.

But Valence is essentially a place for a short stop, or to use as a base of a few days' touring rather than a holiday. It is an important market for all the produce of the Rhône Valley, and is also a centre for jewellery manufacture, precision engineering, packaging and the manufacture of chemical products.

Wine-lovers may like to make the short drive north on the N7 from Valence to **Tain-l'Hermitage**, where one of the best of the often under-estimated wines of the Rhône Valley is produced. Hermitage is a wine made largely from the Syrah grape, which is said to have been brought back from the Middle East by the Crusader Henri Gaspard de Staremberg, who planted it himself near the little chapel at the top of the Hermitage hill, now com-pletely terraced for vine growing. Hermitage became a famous wine far and wide before burgundy was made, and long before the Benedictine monks developed champagne. From the belvedere at the top of the Hermitage hill, 230m above the river, there is a good view of the river valley and across to the hills of Ardèche.

The twin towns of **Romans-sur-Isère** and **Bourg-de-Péage**, which face each other across the Isère, are within an easy drive of Tain-l'Hermitage (via the D532) or of Valence (via the N532). Romans is the chief centre of the French shoe industry. It has an unusual museum devoted to shoes from all parts of the world, from the remotest antiquity — there are even the booted feet of Egyptian mummies — up to the present day, with the weighted boots of the first men who walked on the moon.

It was in the collegial church of St Barnard in Romans that the treaty was signed in 1349 by which the Dauphiné became part of the kingdom of France. The church was rebuilt in the 13th century among the ruins of a 9th-century monastery, some traces of which remain. The columns of the nave have some interesting capitals. The church is famous for the nine 15th-century wall-hangings depicting the Passion of Christ, in the chapel of the St Sacrament on the right hand side of the nave.

From Bourg de Péage the N532 leads east towards St Nazaire-en-Royans and the Parc Regional de Ver-cors. The further you move eastwards away from the plain of Valence and the Rhône, the wilder becomes the countryside of Drôme. The hills be-come larger, the valleys narrower, and everywhere ahead there is the wall of mountains rising away to the Alps. There are great stretches of country where there are hardly any roads. All the important roads, some of them very pretty, follow the river valleys into the mountains.

St Nazaire-en-Royans is a little old town given a great deal of character by its attractive situation at the con-fluence of the Bourne and the Isère and by the 19th-century viaduct which stretches massively but with some elegance across the river. It was built to carry water to the plain of Valence. St Nazaire is very much a small tourist resort. An artificial lake behind a barrage has been developed as a tourist centre. Boat trips are available.

Another good excursion from Valence is to Crest and on from there by the valley of the Drôme to Saillans and Die (not 'dye' but 'dee'). Crest is on the banks of the Drôme where

The viaduct across the Isère at St Nazaire-en-Royans

it comes down from the mountains into the plain. It is a town of limited interest, dominated by the largest castle keep in France, all that is left of the old fortress destroyed on the orders of Louis XIII. The keep is empty apart from one room which contains a collection of weapons. From the upper terrace there is a view over the town and a fine panorama beyond it.

From Crest it is an enjoyable drive along the D93 to Saillans and Pontaix. The small villages of this region special-ise in the production of an unusual wine, sold under the name of Clairette de Die. It is a light, sparkling white with just a hint of the muscat grape in the flavour, and makes a good summer drink. Pontaix is a kind of prototype of dozens of villages in the foothills of

Drôme, Isère and northern Provence, picturesque, immediately beside the river, and backed by conical hill topped by a ruined castle.

Die, a sous-prefecture of Drôme, is beautifully situated in a wide, sunny valley ringed by mountains. It is dry and sheltered from winds, and summers can be torrid. Many peasants have left the land for an easier life in the industries of the Rhône Valley, and those that remain cultivate their vine-yards, grow fields of lavender, which perfume the air for miles, and keep sheep on the mountainsides, and goats whose milk they make into excellent cheese. Die is also the chief centre for the marketing of the Clairette wine.

Die – its name comes from the Roman Dea Augusta – was an

important country town where rich Roman merchants and officials had villas and country estates. Bits of Roman roads, Roman bridges, some still complete, and other Roman remains are scattered throughout the landscape. In Die itself the collapse of the Roman Empire left its mark. In the 3rd century AD, as Barbarian attacks became more frequent, the citizens of Die tore down the many Roman monuments in the town and used the stones to build ramparts against the attackers. Some of these stones, with Roman inscriptions, can still be seen in the walls of old houses, and in the arch of the Porte St Marcel, built into later medieval fortifications. In the chapel of the former bishop's palace, now part of the Town Hall, there is a very unusual mosaic in the style of Gallo-Roman times but dating from the 12th century, which is supposed to represent the Earthly Paradise, and personifies four rivers, including the Tigris and the Euphrates. It is an extremely odd work, more naive and cabbalistic than the more formal styles usually found in mosaic work.

The whole of the charming countryside of the Diois (pronounced 'dee-wah') is recovering from its depopulation with the development of tourism. Many of the villages have their own camp sites, bathing places, and often other tourist facilities. There are small hotels and village restaurants where you can enjoy the local cuisine at prices which are a distant memory in fashionable resorts. It is easy to become attached to these quiet villages, and to return to them year after year. Many of their empty and neglected houses are being acquired and restored as holiday homes.

Going south from Valence (on the N7 or the *autoroute*), the next important town is **Montélimar**. In the past this stretch of the Rhône, from Valence to Montélimar and on to Avignon, suffered repeatedly and drastically from floods, and the nearest towns are often, like Montélimar, distanced from the low and uncertain eastern bank. But the Donzère-Mondragon scheme (p. 17) and others have changed all that, and also provided the power that has transformed the life of the Rhône Valley, attracting all kinds of industry.

But Montélimar, though it now has diversified industry, remains famous for the manufacture of nougat. This began soon after the introduction of the almond tree into France from Asia at the beginning of the 17th century. It was first cultivated by the great French horticulturist Olivier de Serres, on his estate at Villeneuve de Berg, just across the river in Ardèche (See box, p. 86). Over the years more and more almond trees were planted throughout the south. There was also a plentiful supply of honey from Provence and the hills of Drôme, and plenty of eggs on the farms. It was not long before a clever farmer's wife began to make and sell nougat. But it was not until the early part of this century that factories were set up for its manufacture. Until then it was just a cottage industry. One of the longest established of these factories is Chabert and Guillot, which welcomes visits from tourists, explains and demonstrates the methods of manufacture, and offers free samples of the product, which is sold at factory prices.

The name Montélimar is derived from Mont Adhémar, the name given to a fortress built there in the 12th century by the powerful Adhémar family. The château was extended in the 14th century, and partially destroyed and rebuilt on several occasions since. It still exists and is open to the public, mornings and afternoons, except on Tuesdays and Wednesday mornings. It is a good reference for the succeeding forms of military architecture over the years.

The area east of Montélimar is full of picturesque roads and old villages which vie with each other in charm, and a round tour is well worthwhile. Leaving Montélimar by the D540 the first of these attractive villages is reached by a fork to the right on to the D327 and then right again (D126) to Puygiron. This is a neatly restored village dominated by its 13th-century château, and enjoys a splendid position with fine views.

Return from Puygiron to the D540 and continue east to **La Bégude-de-Mazenc**. This little town, now a thriving holiday centre, is one of several examples where the local authorities decided in the 19th century that it would be safe and advantageous to move their village from its old defensive position on a hilltop down to the more convenient plain, with its better roads and communications. Another good example is the village of Allan, on the D126 south of Puygiron, where the old village is a ruin perched above the 'new' village on the main road. At La Bégude-de-Mazenc the old village, sometimes called Vieille Bégude, but more properly called **Châteauneuf-de-Mazenc**, should be visited. Though it is now largely restored, this old village, entered by a fortified gateway, retains much of its medieval character. Its network of

alleys and ancient houses is being given new life by craftsmen and artisans who have installed studios and workshops in the old buildings.

This part of Drôme is known as Drôme Provençal, not only from its nearness to Provence, but because it has the same dry and sunny climate, which is making it increasingly popular as a holiday destination.

From La Bégude the D540 continues through the spacious valley of the Jabron in increasingly attractive scenery. The next village, **Le Poët-Laval** is another example of a relatively modern village on the main road with the old village on the hillside above it. The modern village is of no interest, but it is worth making the short detour to the old village, beautifully situated overlooking the valley. It is dominated by the buildings of a former commanderie of the Knights of Malta, now converted to a small but luxuriously comfortable hotel, with an expensive but really first-class restaurant. The village also has a small museum devoted to the history of Protestantism in the Dauphiné.

The 'capital' of this lovely region is the small town of **Dieulefit**, charmingly situated in a slightly more open part of the valley. It is a town of tree-lined boulevards, shady parks and flowering shrubs, and seems to have the gracious style of a small spa, which it is not. It is, however, a health resort; its pure air and dry, sunny climate have given it a good reputation in the treatment of non-infectious respiratory illness, and as a place for those suffering from stress and overwork to relax. It is a lively and well-equipped centre for tourism with several small hotels, good restaurants, and facilities for camping, swimming,

The older village of Poët Laval has some interesting features, including this medieval gateway

tennis, horse-riding, fishing, and clay pigeon-shooting.

Dieulefit, which is a strongly Protestant town, was founded in the Middle Ages and still has an attractive old quarter called La Viale. The town has a long-established tradition of craftsmanship, particularly in the making of high-grade pottery and glass, and wrought iron. There are also many painters, sculptors, and craftsmen jewellers established in the town.

North of Dieulefit via the D538 is the beautifully situated hill village of **Bourdeaux** which still has the ruins of its feudal castle, and narrow streets graced by some fine Renaissance houses. It has a swimming pool, camp site, and facilities for tennis and fishing – virtually all the rivers in this part of

Drôme are good trout streams. It has a sunny and bracing climate which attracts holidaymakers. On 15 August the village puts on a torchlight historical procession to which spectators come in their thousands from all over the department.

Return to Dieulefit, where the D538 turns east and then south through the valley of the Lez, another scenic route. After about 10km a short turning on the left leads up to the ancient ruined village of Béconne, another example of a village whose inhabitants abandoned it to move down to the plain. The whole of this region is wonderful walking country, and is crossed by two of the Grandes Randonnées national footpaths, the GR9 which, via the mountains of Allans

Evening sun gives an even more romantic air to the 'capital' of Drôme Provençal, Diuelefit

and Les Vaux, links the old village of Béconne to the town of Nyons, a walk of about 20km, and the GR429, which runs westward from the GR9 across wooded hills to the Rhône itself.

The D538 continues down this lovely valley where you turn right on the D14 to the villages of Taulignan and Grignan. It is worth strolling around **Taulignan**, a walled and gated village, with attractive squares and interesting old houses. It is one of several places in the area known for cuisine based on the local truffles. This part of Drôme, together with some parts of Provence, is after Perigord the most important source of the famous truffle in France. In the past two or three years, because of repeated droughts in southern France, truffles

have become more and more scarce. They are 'in season' from October to April, and this winter they are said to have reached 3,000F (£300) per kilo.

Taulignan is only 7km by the D14 from its more famous neighbour, **Grignan**, which can also be reached via the D24 to the delightful old village of Salles-sous-Bois, and then the D56, a slightly longer but more attractive route.

Grignan is built on a small but isolated hill, on the top of which stands the finest Renaissance château in this part of France. This was where the family of Adhémar de Monteil, who also built the château of Montélimar, had their roots. They were already lords of Grignan when Gaucher Adhémar de Monteil began building

129

Madame de Sevigné and Grignan

Marie de Rabutin-Chantal, who as Madame de Sevigné became one of the great names of French literature, was orphaned at seven, and left a widow with two children at 25. After running through her fortune and deceiving her with countless other women, her husband, the Marquis de Sevigné, got himself killed in a duel over a courtesan.

Though she had offers, Madame de Sevigné had had enough of wedded bliss and chose never to marry again. But she was determined that her daughter, Françoise, whom she adored, and called 'the most beautiful girl in France', should marry well.

In 1669, when she was 23, Françoise married the forty-year-old François de Castellane Adhémar de Monteil, Count of Grignan. He was ugly, and she was his third wife. But two years later he became (and remained for forty years) Lieutenant-General (in practice a sort of viceroy) of Provence, based at Grignan.

Madame de Sevigné made several long stays with her daughter at the Château de Grignan, which she liked for its splendour and animated social life. She also enjoyed the superb food. In letters to friends she referred to the delicious partridges stuffed with the herbs of Provence, the fat roast quails, the melons, the figs, the table grapes.

As an over-fond mother, she tended to interfere in the domestic life of her daughter, and for some time the Count banned her from Grignan, though she was later welcomed back.

When she was in her own château near Vitré, in Brittany, Madame de Sevigné wrote frequently to Françoise. Her letters were meant to amuse and entertain, sometimes to inform and advise. When she was at Grignan she wrote to family and friends in other parts of France.

She did not think of herself as a writer, and had no literary pretensions. But her uncle and guardian, the Abbé de Coulanges, had ensured that she had the best possible education. She was fluent in Latin, Spanish, and Italian, and had an exceptional command and knowledge of French. She was familiar with the life of the Court and the nobility, but also loved the country. She had many interests, understood the problems of house and estate management, and read widely. She had the gift of integrating her knowledge naturally into what she wrote. Her letters covered many aspects of human activity, from simple family matters to the lives and deaths of the great. She never prejudiced anyone's reputation, was amusing and sometimes light-hearted, but never sentimental. Above all she had the gift common to all great writers of expressing the deepest truths through simple details.

Madame de Sevigné died at Grignan in 1696, aged 70. Despite her wisdom and love, she and her daughter had never had an easy relationship. It was her grand-daughter, Pauline, who first collected her letters for publication. The first edition appeared in 1734, nearly forty years after her death. They have been in print ever since.

the fortress in the 15th century. When he died in 1516, it was continued by his son, Louis, and finished in 1528. The château was inherited in the following century by François de Castellane Adhémar de Monteil de Grignan – in that period they like names that sounded like a trumpet fanfare – who was Lieutenant General of Provence, and who married, as his third wife, the daughter of the famous Madame de Sevigné (see box).

At the time of the French Revolution, the château belonged to the Comte de Muy, who had bought it from Madame de Sevigné's grand-daughter. It was confiscated by Revolutionary authority and was partially destroyed. The splendid château which the visitor sees today is the results of the efforts of a Madame Fontaine, who bought the château in 1912 and spent seven years restoring it. The impressive southern façade facing Mont Ventoux was rebuilt according to the original plans. Enclosed by two round towers, it consists of three floors, each with tall windows separated by pillars and columns. The western façade opens on to a magnificent terrace enclosed by a balustrade, and this paved terrace forms the roof of the church of St Saveur which adjoins the castle. It affords panoramic views over the rose-coloured roofs of the town across to the distant Vivarais mountains in Ardèche. Even without its literary associations with Madame de Sevigné, the castle would be well worth visiting.

For some years the château has belonged to the Drôme department, whose Office of Works has carried on the restoration, refurbishing the interior and filling it with superb period furniture and works of art.

Festivals of chamber music are held in the castle from February to May, and on summer evenings from July to September there are *son et lumière* shows – at Grignan they call them *fêtes nocturnes*.

Home of Madame de Sevigné, the Château de Grignan

The church of St Sauveur was built in the 1530s but was sacked and badly damaged by Protestant armies during the religious wars thirty years later. It was restored in the middle of the 17th century. Near the main altar, which has a 17th-century carved wooden reredos, are the tombs of the Adhémar de Monteil family, and that of Madame de Sevigné, who died in the château in 1696.

Of the original six gates of the town only one remains, topped by a 17th-century bell turret. The old town around the château still has some vestiges of its ramparts, and in the narrow streets there are restored houses of the 15th, 16th and 17th centuries.

Not far from Grignan there is another very picturesque old village associated with the Adhémar de Monteil family. **La Garde-Adhémar** is a perched village. *Garde* means a promontory and often occurs in place names in this part of France. It is not far from the Rhône itself, and overlooks a long stretch of the valley. The view from the belvedere near the church takes in the whole of the Tricastin, the south-west corner of Drôme, and includes 20th-century elements such as the huge nuclear power station of Tricastin, the great engineering works of the Donzère-Mondragon canal and the Autoroute du Soleil, with the centuries old pattern of vineyards and cultivated fields. The village itself is charming, a place in which to wander and note the rich architectural detail surviving from the past.

La Garde-Adhémar was a walled village but all that remains now of the ramparts is the arched and fortified northern gateway. Another survival is the chapel of the White Penitents, a building which once formed part of the feudal castle, now disappeared. The chapel was recently restored and is now used for audio-visual presentations. On the back wall there is a fresco, officially dated 1710, showing two hooded penitents facing each other on their knees. After the abolition by the Church of public penitence in the Middle Ages, voluntary penitents formed societies whose members took it upon themselves to absolve the sins of others. This they did by nursing the sick and undertaking the burial of the dead during epidemics. One of these societies, known by the colour of their robes, was the White Penitents.

An example of the unpredictability of fate is that, just to the east of the village, there was until the French Revolution a splendid Renaissance château, which rivalled Grignan. Little remains today to suggest the magnificence of the residence of Antoine Escalin, an extraordinary man who started life as a shepherd, became a soldier, an ambassador, then a general and Baron de la Garde. He has been described as *un chevalier sans peur, mais peut etre pas sans reproche* (a knight without fear, but perhaps not without reproach). He died in his castle in 1578, and his château was finally destroyed during the French Revolution, unlike Grignan which has survived in as great a splendour as ever.

But the real jewel of La Garde-Adhémar is its lovely and unusual Romanesque church. It has two apses, one at the eastern end and one at the western, a plan which is very rare in southern France, though sometimes seen in Germany near the Rhine. The church has simple but harmonious lines, and the refinement of the design is emphasised by the quality of the frieze around the western apse. The main altar is believed to be an ancient sacrificial stone.

The fine condition of the church today is due to Prosper Merimée, the well-known French author who was also Minister of Works, and had it restored in 1840. The octagonal tower, with its Romanesque arches and small spire, which goes so well on the original square tower, was added at that time.

Just below the church there is a garden in which hundreds of varieties of aromatic and medicinal plants are cultivated.

La Garde-Adhémar has one small hotel and several good restaurants, and it is an ideal place to make a lunch stop and to explore either before or after the meal. Taking a car into the village in summer is not recommended and it is better to park as close as you can and walk.

Only 2km from La Garde-Adhémar in a cool and rustic spot called the Val des Nymphes there is a ruined Romanesque chapel, mysterious and enchanting, at a place where a spring bubbles from the ground and forms a pool. Its only roof is the blue sky, but what remains, including the façade and the double-arched choir are pure Romanesque in style. The chapel was built in the 12th century by Benedictine monks from the abbey of Tournus in Burgundy, who founded a small community here, perhaps hoping to purify the site which had been used in pagan fertility rites from time immemorial.

Continue south via the D133 or the D158 to **St Paul-Trois-Châteaux**. This

old and pleasant town is still partly surrounded by the remains of its medieval walls, but it has never had three castles. It is the 'capital' of the Tricastin, and its name probably comes from an attempt of a medieval clerk to translate the old Roman name into French. St Paul-Trois-Châteaux has a little-known but superb cathedral, one of the finest Romanesque buildings in southern France. It is a treasure house of architectural detail. The portal suggests an unfinished Roman triumphal arch, which was fitted at the time of Louis XIV with a pair of beautifully carved oak doors. The interior is impressive for the height of the nave, 24m, and the transept is faced with a false triforium above a finely carved frieze. There are 12th- and 13th-century mosaic pavings behind the gilded 17th-century altar.

In the precincts of the cathedral there are a number of restored Renaissance and 18th-century houses. Those interested in gastronomy may like to visit the Maison de la Truffe, attached to the Syndicat d'Initiative near the cathedral, which contains a small museum and exhibition concerning truffles.

From St Paul-Trois-Châteaux the D59 leads to **Suze-la-Rousse**, a pleasant old wine-producing village, whose modest houses are sternly overlooked by a majestic rose-red castle. It dates from the 14th century, but the interior courtyard and apartments were elaborately restored in Renaissance times. The courtyard, with its elegant arches below two floors of tall mullioned windows, separated by fluted columns and pillars, and with a wealth of typical Renaissance embellishment, finely sculpted coats of arms, assertive gargoyles, and elegant balustrades, is

The 14th-century château at Suze-la-Rousse now houses a 'university of wine'

a surprising contrast with the earlier rugged military architecture of the castle's exterior.

There is another Suze in Drôme, Suze-sur-Crest, not to be confused with Suze-la-Rousse, which is said to get its name not from the rose-red castle but from a Comtesse de Suze in medieval times whose reputation matched her flaming red hair.

From Suze the D94 leads east towards the mountains and brings you to **Nyons**, a delightful small town. Though it is in Drôme, Nyons is in every way Provençal, a town of the Mediterranean south. It lies where the valley of the Eygues widens into a sunny bowl protected by mountains,

so that Nyons enjoys a particularly favourable climate, with mild winters and hot summers. All the tender plants of the Riviera grow out of doors here all year round.

The town has a very old part known as the *quartier des Forts*, which has a number of 14th-century houses and the rue des Grands Forts, like a covered gallery, and there are other covered passages known as *soustets* linking the narrow streets. Apart from this fascinating old quarter Nyons also has a remarkable 13th-century bridge still in use. It is a single steep arch of fine proportions spanning the Eygues.

Nyons is famous for its olives, which like good wines have been given their own *appellation controlée*. The groves around the town emphasise its Provençal character. Those who like olive oil will enjoy a short tour of one of the mills where production methods are demonstrated and explained, such as the Moulin d'Autran near the river. There is also a small museum devoted to the olive, showing the tools and equipment used in traditional cultivation, and old and new methods of producing the oil.

There is a fine market place with 14th-century arcades, and many interesting old buildings scattered through the town. Nyons is one of those fortunate places which is not only interesting, but which with its lovely climate, clear air, silver light and superb setting, has a magnetic charm. Many people who spend a holiday there tend to get drawn back, and then return year after year, and perhaps buy a second home or retire there.

In addition to olives, Nyons is a centre for truffles, lavender, lime flowers and orchard fruits. It was not without reason that Jean Giono, one of the best known authors of the Midi, who knew the whole of Provence, said, 'All this lovely countryside of happy hills and silver light touches me in the depths of my heart. Nyons seems to me to be the earthly paradise.'

Having got as far as Nyons it is well worth visiting the neighbouring region called the Baronnies, named from the fact that in medieval times the land was shared between the barons of Montbrun, Mevouillon, and Montauban. In the 14th century they sold out to the Dauphin, and the district became the south-eastern limit of the Dauphiné. Although it has three

rivers, the Eygues, the Ouvèze, and the Méouge, the Baronnies is hot, sunny and dry, and in places almost desert. Myrtle, lavender, terebinth, and other aromatic plants grow wild on the sun-baked hillsides. But the dry soil is often difficult to cultivate, and in the past 150 years two-thirds of the peasant population have moved away.

The Baronnies is wonderful country for those who like old villages, picturesque châteaux and remnants of all the art in stone that flowered in the Middle Ages and classical times. The road from Nyons is the D538 to the south through Mirabel-aux-Baronnies to La Tuilière, which is actually in Provence, where you turn left on to the D46 through Puymeras to **Mollans-sur-Ouvèze**. This is a really pretty village, just away from the foot of Mont Ventoux, with an ancient bridge over the river and a fortified tower, an unusual arcaded wash house, and an old fountain in the middle of the village. It is one of the centres of the gentle tourism which is helping to revive the economy of the Baronnies. It is a mecca for fishing, walking, cycling, and has a leisure centre, Pas de Ventoux, with accommodation, swimming pool, tennis, and restaurant, as well as small hotels, a camp site and cottages for rent.

From Mollans the road follows the valley of the Ouvèze to Buis-les-Baronnies, the traditional 'capital' of the region. The Ouvèze, which eventually joins the Rhône just north of Avignon, is a well-known trout stream, and from Mollans onwards the whole of its valley is scenically beautiful. Just beyond Mollans on the way to Buis-les-Baronnies you pass the village of Pierrelongue, easily recognised by its church built on top of an isolated rock, encircled by a spiral footpath — looking like a smaller version of the famous chapel of St Martin-d'Aiguilhe in Le Puy.

Buis-les-Baronnies is another delightful town with a long past. It has an old quarter, an old bridge, a market place with 15th-century arcades and a 12th-century tower.

After the heat of the day both tourists and locals sit long into the summer evenings in the shade of massive plane trees, planted in 1811 as a gift from the Emperor Napoleon to celebrate the birth of his son, the ill-fated King of Rome, who died at twenty-one. Buis-les-Baronnies is the most important market for lime flowers, which make the lime infusion popular in France, and also produces olives, almonds and orchard fruit. It is becoming increasingly popular with tourists, and has a municipal swimming pool and facilities for hill walking on signposted footpaths, rock climbing, pony trekking, fishing, and other outdoor activities. There are hotels and restaurants, camp sites, and a naturist holiday camp.

It is too far from the Rhône here for the mistral to be felt, and the region has a superb climate. It is not, perhaps, the place for tourists who look for luxury and sophistication, but for those happy with reasonable comfort, good food, lovely surroundings, and above all the freedom to make their own discoveries, the Baronnies will not disappoint. The surrounding hills and mountains are wild, remote and sun-baked, but for the visitor there is always another ancient town, another ruined castle, another tiny village apparently locked in time, another old Romanesque church, waiting to be discovered, or perhaps just an unforgettable picnic spot beside a sparkling stream.

Hotels & Restaurants

Prices: A = Very Expensive, B = Expensive, C = Moderately Expensive, D = Average, E = Cheap.

BUIS-LES-BARONNIES (26170 Drôme): **Le Saint-Marc** at Mollans-sur-Ouvèze (75 28 70 01). Sound regional restaurant. Meals D–E. Rooms plain and simple: Rooms E. Well situated at the foot of Mont Ventoux.

DIE (26150 Drôme): **Relais de Chamarges**, av de la Clairette (75 22 00 95). Standard Logis de France, 1km outside town. Good regional restaurant. Rooms E. Meals E.

DIEULEFIT (26220 Drôme): **L'Escargot d'Or**, route de Nyons (75 46 40 52). Attractive family-run Logis just outside the town. Simple, unpretentious rooms and restaurant, but the patron is a first-class chef. Swimming pool. Rooms E. Meals E.

LA GARDE-ADHEMAR (26700 Pierrelatte, Drôme): **Le Tisonnier** (75 04 44 03). Excellent restaurant with emphasis on fish dishes, in a delightful old village. Reservation advised. Not cheap but excellent value. Meals C.

MONTÉLIMAR (26740 Drôme): **Lou Mas**, pl des Ecoles, L'Homme d'Armes (75 01 90 83), 2km north of Montélimar via the N7. Good, welcoming restaurant. Fresh produce, menus changed daily. Meals D–E.

NYONS (26110 Drôme): **La Picholine**, promenade de la Perrière (75 26 06 21). Simple but spacious Logis in an ancient olive grove outside the town. Some rooms overlooking the pool. Rooms and meals D–D+.
Auberge du Vieux Village d'Aubres (75 26 12 89). Magnificently sited above the old village of Aubres 3km from Nyons. Panoramic views from the terrace and the dining room (no smoking). Restaurant with good food but fixed hours. Rooms and meals B.
Le Colombet, 83 pl de la Liberation (75 26 03 66). Good traditional southern restaurant, good value at reasonable prices. Also a hotel, for those who do not mind being in the middle of a small town, very good. Rooms D–E. Meals C–E.

PIERRELATTE (26700 Drôme): **Les Recollets**, 6 pl de l'Eglise (75 96 83 10). Pleasant, simple, impeccably run restaurant, tasty dishes at modest prices. Meals C–E.

LE POËT-LAVAL (26160 La Bégude-de-Mazenc, Drôme): **Les Hospitaliers** (75 46 22 32). In a medieval village, once a stronghold of the Knights of St John of Jerusalem, 4km from Dieulefit. Exceptional in every way. Not spacious but luxurious, period furniture and paintings. Restaurant with terrace and lovely views. Even the table settings are works of art. Superb food. Small swimming pool. Rooms and meals B–C.

SUZE-LA-ROUSSE (26790 Drôme): **Relais du Château** (75 04 87 07). Quiet situation on edge of village next to vineyards. Fairly new Logis de France, well run, with good restaurant. Swimming pool. Tennis. Rooms D. Meals D–E.

Château de Rochegude (75 04 81 88). A Relais et Châteaux hotel on a rocky height overlooking the plain of the Rhône. At Rochegude, 14km north of Orange, just across the border in Drôme. Impressive interior, high degree of comfort, and good restaurant. Rooms and meals B–C.

VALENCE (26000 Drôme): **Pic**, 285 av Victor Hugo (75 44 15 32). Another one of the really great restaurants of France to be found in the Rhône Valley. Reigned over by Jacques Pic and son, Alain, in an atmosphere of professional calm and unsurpassed quality. Closed Wed, Sun evenings, and 1 to 26 August. There are also two elegant apartments, and two sumptuous bedrooms. Prices are high but about two-thirds of what the same quality would cost in Paris or Cannes. Rooms B. Meals A.

Hotel 2000, av de Romans (75 43 73 01). Modern hotel in a quiet situation just outside town, on the road to Grenoble. Comfortable rooms, good service. Restaurant with terrace. Rooms C–D. Meals D.

Ibis, 385 av de Provence (75 44 42 54). One of the reliable modern chain, at the exit from the autoroute. Functional but good value. Soundproofed rooms. Restaurant by swimming pool. Rooms D. Meals D.

Museums, Châteaux etc: opening times

Note: am/pm means closed for lunch (normally for two hours).

VALENCE: Museum (red chalk drawings), am/pm Wed, Sat and Sun, pm only other days of the week. Closed on public holidays.

ROMANS-SUR-ISERE: Shoe Museum, am/pm Mon–Sat, pm Sun. Closed Tues.

MONTÉLIMAR: Château, am/pm. Closed Tues and Wed am.

GRIGNAN: Château. Accompanied visits (half, one, or one and a half hours) am/pm. Closed Tues and Wed am (except in July and Aug). *Son et lumière* spectacle from mid-July to mid-Sept.

SUZE-LA-ROUSSE: Château. Accompanied visits in the afternoon. Closed Tues.

NYONS: Moulin Autrand, am/pm. Closed Sun and second fortnight of Oct. **Museum of Olives**. Open Sat pm from Easter to end of Sept and Thurs and Fri pm as well in July and Aug.

Leisure

ROCK CLIMBING Information from M. Mailhe, Club de l'Escalade Buxois, Buis-les-Baronnies, 26710, Drôme. Or from Syndicat d'Initiative, pl Champ de Mars.

HORSE-RIDING More than two dozen centres. Details from La Drôme a Cheval, 21 rue de Royan, Romans-sur-Isère, 26100, Drôme.

CANOE-KAYAK Ask at the nearest tourist information office.

Tourist Information Office

VALENCE — pl Leclerc.

Scale
0   10   20   30   40km

- N --

Pont-St-Esprit

R. Eygues

Ruines Romaines
R. Ouveze

Roaix

Vaison-la-Romaine

Bagnols-S-Cèze

Camaret-
S. Aigues

Arc
de
Triomphe

Malaucène

Mont Ventoux

D6

N580

N86

D975

Orange

Théâtre Antique

D976

Roquemaure

Châteauneuf-
du-Pape

Carpentras

D981

Uzès

Villeneuve-les-
Avignon

Sorgues

D938

N106

Remoulins

D225

A7

Fontaine-de-Vaucluse

Pont-du-Gard

N100

AVIGNON

D986

N7

D25

R. Rhone

Châteaurenard

D19A

D371

N538

Cavaillon

NÎMES

Beaucaire

Tarascon

St. Rémy-
de-Provence

D27

Les Antiques/St. Paul-de-Mausole
Ruines de Glanum

A9

N113

N86

N570

Chaîne des Alpilles

Les Baux-
de-Provence

D973

St. Gilles

D17

D17

ARLES

N113

Salon-de-Provence

N572

D570

Plaine de la Camargue

Plaine de la Crau

D10

N113

A7

Étang de
Vaccarès

D35

N568

D5

Istres

Pont
de Gau

Parc
Ornithologique

Stes. Maries-de-la-Mer

Martigues

Gulf du Lion

140

9
Around Avignon

There has always been a touch of magic, an almost hypnotic attraction, about Provence. For the Romans it was Provincia, their promised land on the other side of the Alps. For the Gauls in the rest of France, and later for all the peoples of northern Europe, this dry, sunny, and beautiful area beside a timeless sea had the fascination of the exotic. Like Spain, Provence seems in many ways more an outpost of Africa than part of Europe. Protected from the north and east by mountains, Provence, especially near the Mediterranean shore, has a warmer climate than other parts of France. Its natural vegetation is a scrub of spiky and aromatic bushes, and what grows in North Africa also grows in Provence, from cactus to oranges and lemons.

If the natural vegetation is different, so are the people. The congenial climate has produced a race of easy-going, jovial, independent people with their own language, their own customs and their own history. Tourists tend to think of Provence as a strip of sunlit, scenic coast beside a deep blue sea, but that is only a small part of the whole. Modern Provence, which is only the eastern half of the Roman Provincia, is still a large area, reaching 150km inland. Most of it is upland or mountain, apart from the Rhône

Valley, and it is this part of Provence, with its ancient towns and less familiar tourist destinations, that this chapter describes.

From the visitor's point of view there are two main attractions, the beautiful and often spectacular scenery, and an unequalled number of Roman and medieval sites.

It is surprising how few people familiar with the Roman sites of Vienne, Orange, Nîmes, and Arles have visited **Vaison-La-Romaine**, which has an excavated section of a Roman town covering more than thirty acres in a park-like setting, as well as a Roman theatre.

Vaison is only just across the border from the department of Drôme and is easily reached from Grignan (D941, D938), St Paul-Trois-Châteaux (D59, D94, D20), Suze-la-Rousse (D94, D20) or Nyons (D538). In Roman times it was an important administrative centre. The remains of patrician houses, shopping streets, baths, and a Roman public garden, in addition to the theatre, make it easy to imagine the town as it must have been.

The ruins are in two parts, the Quartier Puymin on one side of the main road, and the Quartier Villasse on the other, and there is a public car park between the two. The Quartier

Statue of the Empress Sabine at
Vaison-la-Romaine

Puymin includes Pompey's Portico, a colonnade, originally roofed, which was a public promenade and garden. Only the north side has been excavated and along this wall there are copies of marble statues found when the theatre was being excavated. The originals are now in the museum on the site. They include the Emperor Hadrian, and his wife, Sabine. Others are of Tiberius, Caligula, and Domitian.

The finest statue ever found at Vaison was discovered by accident near Pompey's Portico, before any serious archaeological work had been done on the site. It is a superbly modelled figure of a young Greek athlete holding a laurel crown above his head. It is known as the Diadumenos, and is in the British Museum.

The Roman theatre, set in the north flank of the hill, is similar to the one at Orange, but is smaller and has no stage wall surviving.

The Quartier Puymin also includes the ruins of a group of workers' houses and the villa of Messius, a patrician, where a fine head of Venus wearing a laurel wreath was found. This head, more statues, and many other things found on the site, including tools, toys, pottery, oil lamps, jewellery, vases, weapons, glassware and Roman money, are exhibited in the museum, which is best visited after a complete tour of the site.

The Quartier Villasse includes part of the paved main road of the Roman town, with the main drain running beneath it and part of the public baths. Just next to the main road was a narrow shopping street, lined with pillars, and at the end of this street, opposite the baths, was the entrance to the villa called the House of the Silver Bust. This house is a good pointer to the lifestyle of wealthy Roman citizens. It covers 3,000m², about 30 times the floor area of a typical modern town house, and included two pillared courtyards with fountains and gardens. The silver bust, probably that of the owner, is now in the museum.

Vaison also has a Roman bridge across the Ouvèze, a solid and inelegant structure, but functional. Apart from repairs to the parapet, it is as it was 2,000 years ago, and is still in daily use. Before crossing this bridge to see the medieval town of Vaison, built on a hill on the other side of the Ouvèze, visitors may like to see the cathedral. Notre-Dame-de-Nazareth is a good example of the Provençal Romanesque style, but has been much restored. There are 11th-century cloisters, restored a hundred years ago.

The medieval town, built originally in the 13th and 14th centuries was, like many other hill towns in this part of France, abandoned in the early 19th century, when the safety of a hilltop became less important than the convenience of the valley. In recent years many of its late medieval and Renaissance houses have been privately restored. Old streets like the rue des Fours, and the old market place, make it worth a look round. From the ruined château above the town, reached by an awkward path, there is a good view of the valley of the Ouvèze, and of Mont Ventoux.

Vaison-la-Romaine is well known for its roses, and the best time to visit the Roman ruins is in early summer, when the roses blooming among the marble pillars and white stones, against a background of pines and green lawns, make it seem like a garden.

To reach the summit of **Mont Ventoux** (1,912m) take the D938 from Vaison to Malaucène, and then the D974, which winds its way upwards along the north flank of the mountain and after about 20km of beautiful route with some magnificent views gets to the top. During summer the

trip is best made early in the morning as in the heat of the day the view in all directions is often spoiled by heat haze. In clear weather Mont Blanc and other Alpine peaks can be seen to the north-east; to the west Monts Mezenc and Gerbier de Jonc can be picked out among the heights of the Massif Central. To the south-west are the valleys of the Rhône and the Durance, and the plain of Provence stretching away to the Etang de Berre, Arles, the Camargue and its lagoons, and the Mediterranean.

The whole area around the slopes of Mont Ventoux is excellent country for the walker, and is crossed by the GR4, GR91 and GR91b national footpaths. There are also facilities for pony trekking and shorter horse rides. The upper slopes and summit of Mont Ventoux should be avoided by all tourists, including motorists, when the mistral is blowing or forecast. It is a positively dangerous as well as nerve-wracking wind. Fortunately it is unusual in summer months.

From Vaison-la-Romaine to Orange is only 20km via the D975 through Roaix and Camaret-sur-Aygues. **Orange** is a small town whose past was a good deal more significant than is its present. It is now a commercial centre and market place for the produce of the region and has a few factories. It has been saved from obscurity and has been given a tourist industry because it has two of the most remarkable Roman monuments in the world, the theatre and the triumphal arch.

Situated directly on the northern approach to the town, the triumphal arch is believed to have been built in the time of Augustus and was dedicated later (c.AD25) to the Emperor Tiberius. It is a remarkable survival;

not the largest existing but the lively decoration, recalling military and naval victories, is in an exceptional state of preservation. A triumphal arch, but what triumph? No scholar has yet attempted to relate it to any particular Roman victory, but it is interesting that Orange was the setting in 105BC for one of the most comprehensive defeats ever suffered by the Roman legions. Two complete Roman armies were routed by an army of Barbarians from the north. It may be supposed that Orange remained a sore spot in Roman tradition, and that when things went more successfully and Orange was allotted to the Second Legion in recognition of its victories, the raising of the arch formed part of this recognition. The arch is best preserved on the northern side and it has been suggested that this is due to the fact that the mistral blowing from the north, is a dry wind which hardens and preserves the stone, whereas the wind from the south, moist and salt-laden, slowly wears it away. The arch was damaged in the Middle Ages, when it was made to serve as a fort, but was carefully restored at the beginning of the 19th century.

The other important site in Orange is the Roman theatre, the only one in Europe which still has its stage wall.

The famous Roman Triumphal Arch, Orange

144

This enormous structure, 103m long and 37m high, also forms the exterior façade of the theatre. Built of huge blocks of stone without the use of mortar, it stands by its own weight, and like the Pont du Gard is, in its solidity and strength, an unforgettable reminder of the genius of Rome. On the stage side this wall was originally ornamented with pillars and friezes, of which little now remains, and with niches in which statues were placed. The theatre was built in the time of the Emperor Augustus and the central and largest niche contained his statue. When the theatre was being restored some years ago this statue was found in pieces in the ditch beneath the wall and was carefully pieced together and replaced in its niche in 1951.

Seating was arranged in a semicircle of 37 tiers divided into three sections, and with the best seats nearest the stage reserved for VIPs. Altogether there were seats for between 9,000 and 10,000 spectators. It is interesting that the stage was protected by a roof and that a ditch ran across the front of it from which a curtain could be raised and lowered.

The acoustics are as good as ever. When I was last there, two small boys about eight or nine years old, being given an educational outing by their father, stood centre stage and sang, with some timidity, *Sur le pont*

The Roman theatre is the most impressive of the Roman sites in Orange

d'Avignon, and from where I was, on the top tier of the auditorium, every word was clear.

Every summer important festivals of music and grand opera are held in the theatre and attract top singers and musicians from all over the world.

Like most Roman theatres, this one is set in a hillside. In Orange a public park has been laid out on top of the hill. It can be reached by car via the rue des Princes d'Orange, west of the theatre complex.

Avignon can be reached directly from Orange by the autoroute or by the N7 with equal ease, about 30km in either case. But wine lovers may prefer to leave Orange by the D976 in the direction of Roquemaure and then turn left on to the D17 for Châteauneuf-du-Pape. On the pleasant country roads around this village there are numerous properties offering the chance to taste and buy the fine wines of the region. The D17 continues to Sorgues, where you take the N7 to Avignon.

The special character of Avignon, which has made it one of the great tourist destinations of Europe, is the product of a number of unusual factors. The town is situated on the left bank of the Rhône at a point where the long green island of Barthelasse divides the river into two channels, and at the foot of the impressive Rocher des Doms, on the slopes of which stand the cathedral and the Palace of the Popes. The charm of this site is best seen from the other side of the river from one of the vantage points in Villeneuve-les-Avignon.

Avignon was an important Roman town but unlike most of the others in

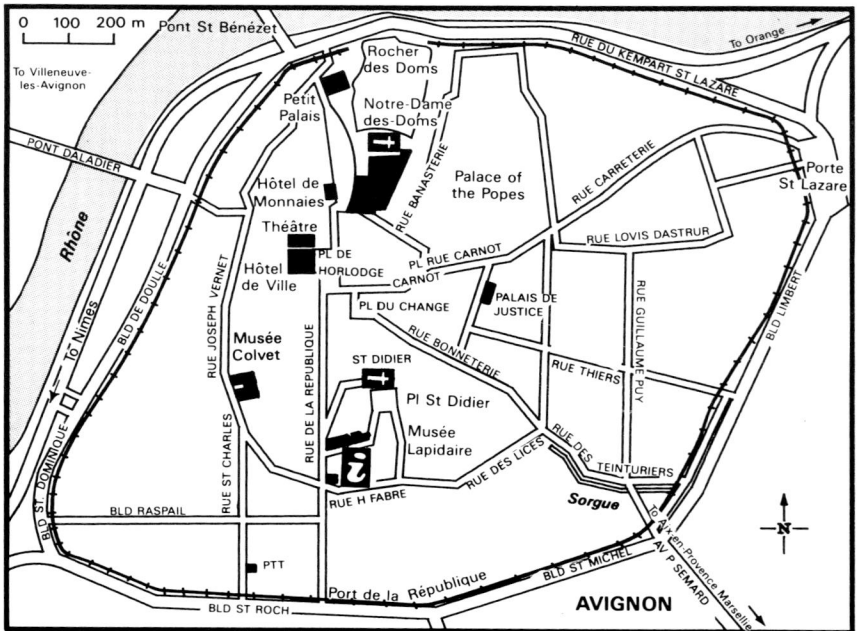

the Rhône Valley, it has no Roman remains, the medieval town having completely buried the Roman site. Again unlike many other old towns in this part of France, where the medieval ramparts were torn down to be replaced by a wide boulevard encircling the town, Avignon still has its entire medieval walls. In Avignon the exterior boulevard encircles the town outside the walls, now pierced by eleven gates, seven of them original, and four modern. It is only the town inside the ramparts which is of any interest to the visitor.

The factor which makes Avignon unique is that for almost 100 years it replaced Rome as the residence of the popes. In the late 13th century Rome was a lawless city, overrun by brigands and thieves, where there were frequent riots, and where no one, least of all the popes with all their treasure, felt safe. In the early 14th century the pope, Clement V, was French by birth. As Bertrand de Got, he had been Archbishop of Bordeaux. The College of Cardinals was also almost entirely French, and the Church owned a part of France, called the Comtat Venaissin, near Avignon, which it had received from the French king in return for help in the crusade against the Albigensian heretics in south-west France at the beginning of the 13th century. Clement V decided to move away from the troubles of Rome and establish the Holy See in the Comtat Venaissin. The move took place in 1309, and Clement V resided at Malaucène, and sometimes at Carpentras. He also made several stays at the Dominican monastery in Avignon, outside the Comtat, which then belonged to the Kingdom of Naples and Sicily.

When Clement V died, the cardinals were unable to agree on a successor. After two years of fierce argument they elected a man of 72, who appeared to be in poor health, as a stop-gap. But Jacques Arnaud Dueze, who called himself John XXII, confounded the cardinals. He not only outlived almost all those who had elected him — he was 91 when he died — but proved to be a great administrator and a financial genius with the golden touch.

When he died he left 20 million gold florins and 7 million in plate and jewels in the papal treasury. It was John XXII who decided to move the papacy from the Comtat Venaissin to Avignon, where he had formerly been bishop. He set about extending the bishop's palace into something more suited to a pope, and also built himself a castle not far from Avignon and planted vineyards around it, so establishing Châteauneuf-du-Pape and its famous wines. He was the first of six French popes who succeeded Clement in France. His successor, Benedict XII, started the construction of a new papal palace, and it was finished by his successor, Clement VI.

It was also Clement VI who bought Avignon from Queen Jeanne of Naples and Sicily, in what in retrospect seems to have been a remarkable piece of wheeler dealing (see box). Once the town belonged to them the popes began to take more care of it, and it was Innocent VI who in the 1350s surrounded the town with new walls.

Despite the fact that Avignon suffered disastrously from the Black Death in 1348 and again in 1361, when 20,000 people died, the town prospered under the popes. In 1376 Pope Gregory XI, largely persuaded

147

The Voluptuous Queen

In the middle of the 14th century Pope Clement VI was happily installed in his newly built palace at Avignon, but the city itself did not belong to the Papacy. It belonged to Queen Jeanne of Naples, Countess of Provence.

By all accounts Queen Jeanne was an opulent beauty, charming as well as voluptuous, but did she order her first husband's brutal murder? Brought up in the most polished and libertine court in Europe, she was married early to a doltish Hungarian prince whom she found it impossible to live with. On 18 September 1345, this Prince Andrew, who was to be elevated to rank of King Consort two days later, was set upon and hanged from a balcony of the summer palace at Aversa.

Was the 20-year-old Queen Jeanne a party to the murder? Petrarch believed her innocent. Nostradamus 'knew' she was guilty. Prince Louis of Hungary, brother of the murdered man, charged Jeanne with murder, and she was arraigned before the Papal Court. But Jeanne was not merely sexy and beautiful, she was extremely clever. She was as fine a classical scholar as any old professor at the Sorbonne, and her Latin was eloquent. She defended herself with charm and energy, and no doubt it was sheer coincidence that she was willing to sell the city of Avignon to Clement VI at a bargain basement price, and that Clement and the Curia were able to declare with confidence that she was innocent. As a bonus, Clement declared the handsome Prince Louis of Taranto, whom Jeanne had married in secret after her first husband's unfortunate death, Count of Provence and King of Jerusalem.

It was not long before Jeanne was accused of infidelity by her new husband and was brutally assaulted, but, in circumstances which have never been questioned, she found herself a widow again. She was married for the third time, to King Jaime of Majorca, who was adored by her, and was handsome but also rather mad, having been kept in an iron cage for 13 years in his youth. Widowed again, she married Otto of Brunswick, a dashing captain of mercenaries, one of the notorious *condottiere* of the Middle Ages. She was widowed again.

In 1381 Louis of Hungary achieved his long-delayed vengeance. He kidnapped Jeanne and imprisoned her in a castle in Basilicata. Nearly 40 years after his brother's murder, Louis sent four Hungarian soldiers to her cell, where she was kneeling at prayer. They strangled her.

by St Catherine of Siena, decided to return to Rome, bringing to an end the 70-year reign of the popes in France. The death of Gregory XI was followed by a period in which the papacy was contested. As in these days different associations or boards recognise different world heavyweight boxing champions, there were different candidates for the Holy See; popes, and anti-popes — at one time there were three popes. Clement VII supported by Charles V of France returned to Avignon. He was succeeded by an equally illegal pope Benedict XIII, who was not in favou-

hands and feet cut off as a punishment for his presumption. But according to the legend, Bénézet demonstrated his divine inspiration by picking up a block of stone 'not less than 4m long and 2m wide' and carrying it on his shoulder to the river bank where he dropped it at the point where he meant to start the foundations of the bridge. Not surprisingly, this action silenced all argument. Not only that, everyone wanted to be a part of this miraculous undertaking, and money poured in from all sides. That is the legend, but there are always those around ready to spoil a good story, and some authorities assert that all St Bénézet did was to form a brotherhood of bridge-building friars, the Frères Pontifex, and set about repairing a Roman bridge already in existence. In any case, St Bénézet died in 1184, four years before the work was completed. His bones were placed in a small chapel erected on the bridge itself, and dedicated to St Nicholas, the patron saint of bridge-builders. The chapel is still there, but the tomb of St Bénézet is now in the church of St Didier.

The bridge was damaged on several occasions during the many attacks on Avignon in medieval times. It was restored in 1410 and continued in use until 1668, when most of its arches were washed away in one of the violent floods of the Rhône.

After these major sights, perhaps the greatest attraction for many tourists is Avignon's atmosphere of racy animation. It is a lively city at all times, but in summer when it is the setting for an international festival of drama, the colourful atmosphere reaches a peak. Music, ballet and drama performances attract spectators from all over Europe, the Far East and America. Groups of strolling players, street musicians and buskers, add their unofficial contributions to the gaiety, and at times it all seems somewhat overdone, and verging on the hysterical.

Even outside the festival season Avignon in summer is crowded and with its sunshine, lively cafés, and outdoor life, it is always pleasant to stroll in. The best place to park is in the underground car park beneath the place du Palais, in front of the Palace of the Popes. Enter Avignon by the Porte de la République, and carry straight on down the main street, the rue de la République, to the end and follow the signs to the car park. It may be a slow business getting there, but it is well signposted and there is usually space.

The church of St Pierre, not far from the Palace of the Popes, has a pair of remarkably fine Renaissance doors, beautifully carved, installed in 1551, but the church itself is open to the public only on Sunday mornings.

St Didier is an older church in the Provençal Gothic style with a single nave with chapels on each side, and a five-sided apse. It has some 14th-century frescos and a 15th-century reredos. It is open to the public in the late afternoon.

Some of the most interesting streets of old Avignon are in the area between these two churches. The rue des Lices, the rue de la Masse, and the rue du Roi René all have some good Renaissance mansions. At the end of the rue du Roi René is the rue des Teinturiers (Dyers' Row), a cobbled

Overleaf: *The famous 'Pont d'Avignon', named after St Bénézet*

151

street beside a narrow branch of the Sorgue, shaded by plane trees. Until the end of the 19th century calicos were made and dyed here for the shawl industry. Some of the old paddle wheels which drove the machines in the mills can still be seen.

As everybody is aware, dignitaries of the Church, however spiritual they may be, are not necessarily laggards when it comes to looking after their bodily comforts. Life in Avignon in the 14th century was as active and noisy as it is today, and for the sake of peace and quiet rich cardinals often moved across the river to what is now Villeneuve-les-Avignon, where they built themselves luxurious retreats. There were originally 15 of these magnificent houses, called *livrées*, and even after the popes and the cardinals left Avignon, Villeneuve retained its exclusivity, and more splendid mansions were built there. But the display of wealth angered the revolutionaries, and these private palaces were sacked and razed during the Revolution. Only three remain.

In the Middle Ages the Rhône marked the boundary between France and part of the Holy Roman Empire. Villeneuve-les-Avignon was in France, and Avignon a republic within the Empire. With the object of keeping an eye on the doings of papacy and Empire, Philippe IV of France built a watch tower at his end of the pont St Bénézet. A spiral staircase leads in 176 apparently interminable steps to a terrace with superb views in all directions.

Villeneuve is on the hill of St André, sometimes called Mont Andaon, a commanding position. Fifty years after Philippe, Kings Jean le Bon and Charles V followed his line of thought

and fortified the top of the hill around the 10th century Benedictine Abbaye St André. There are fine views from the abbey garden, and even better from the terrace of the west tower of the ruined fort.

Avignon is the best base from which to explore this inland part of Provence. Nîmes, the Pont du Gard, Orange, St Rémy and Les Baux, the Fontaine de Vaucluse and Arles are all within easy reach for excursions.

Nîmes, west of the Rhône, and 40km from Avignon via the N100 to Remoulins and then the N86 or the A9 autoroute is a busy and rapidly expanding city, whose population is very largely Protestant. Driving and parking in Nîmes can present problems, but it is worth making the effort because it has two of the finest monuments of the Roman world, the amphitheatre or arena, and the Maison Carrée.

Though there are several larger Roman arenas still in existence, that at Nîmes is in the best state of preservation. It is a shade smaller than the one at Arles, though both could seat about 24,000 spectators, but in other respects it is almost identical, apart from minor details of decoration. In Roman times it was used for a wide variety of spectacles, most of them bloody. These even included mock sea battles – the podium surrounding the arena was watertight and it could be filled with water. The fighting was real enough and combatants were often drowned. But this same wall was not high enough to prevent a lion or a leopard springing out of the arena, so it is not likely that gladiatorial combats against such animals were staged here; at Arles this wall was higher. But fights between gladiators

Tour Magne

Costelium
Le Fort

RUE MENARD

Mont Cavalier

BLD GAMBETTA

To Avignon

BLD SENTENAC

RUE NATIONALE

Temple de Diane

PL
ANTONIN

Jardin de
la Fontaine

QUAI DE LA FONTAINE

Maison
Carree

Cathedrale
Notre-Dame
et St. Castor

BLD ADMIRAL COURBET

RUE DES CHASSAINTES

RUE DE LA
MADELEINE

Old
Quarter

PL DES GREFFES

RUE NOTRE DAME

200m

RUE ROUSSY

AV JEAN JAURES

RUE EMILE JAMAIS

RUE PORTE DE FRANCE

BLD VICTOR HUGO

PL DU
MARCHE

BLD DE
LA LIBERATION

ESPLANADE CHARLES
DE GAULLE

RUE REBOUT

Arena

AV DE CADEREAU

RUE DE L'HÔTEL DIEU

AVE FEUCHERES

To Arles

RUE DU CIRQUE ROMAIN

Musée des
Beaux-Arts

RUE CITE FOUL

RUE DE ST GILLES

PL
SÉVERINE

RUE DE LA REPUBLIQUE

RUE HENRI IV

BLD SERGENT TRIARE

N

RUE DHUODA

To Montpellier

NÎMES

0   100   200 m

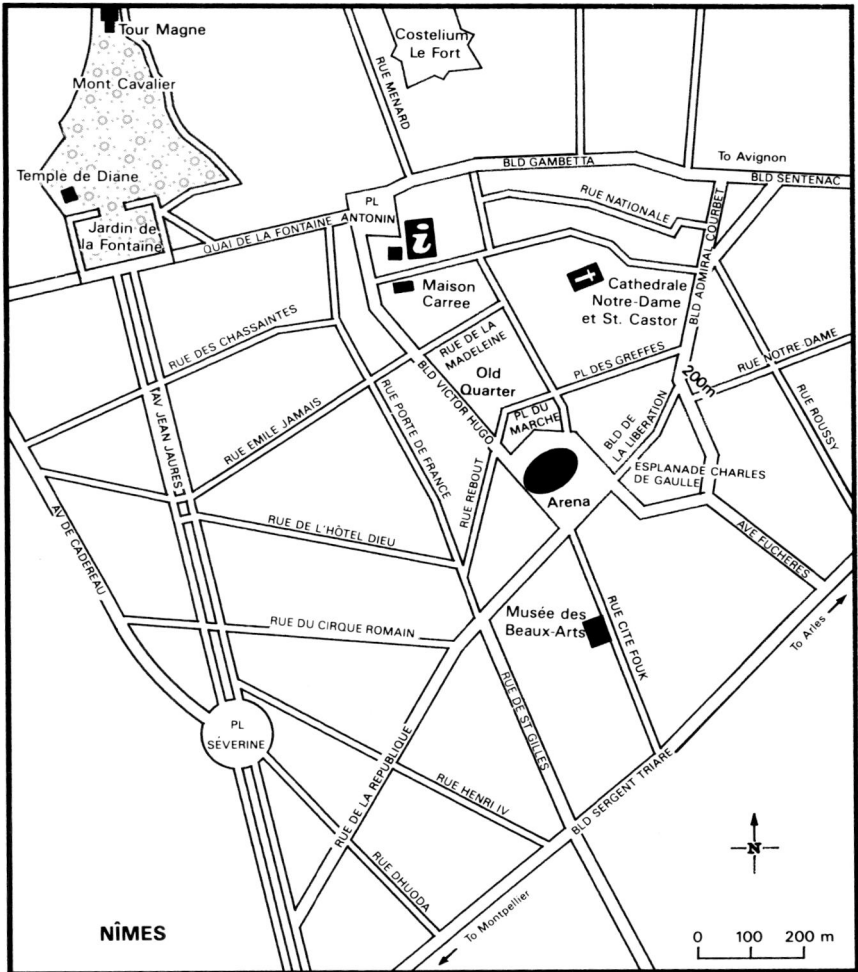

certainly took place, and so did public executions. Combats of all kinds were accompanied by an orchestra to heighten the more dramatic moments, rather as in the days of silent films an energetic pianist battered out a crescendo as the hero galloped after the villain across the plains of the old West.

Today the amphitheatre is in regular use from May to September for bull-fights, some in the Spanish fashion, and some according to Provençal rules, under which the bull is not killed.

The other major sight in Nîmes is the Maison Carrée, the best example of a Roman temple still in existence

One of the greatest Roman sites in Provence, the amphitheatre at Nîmes

in France. It was built during the reign of Augustus, and has 30 Corinthian columns with ornate capitals. It is not large, 26m long by 15m wide and 17m high above its podium.

One visitor to Nîmes in the late 18th century was a gentleman farmer named Arthur Young, who later became in effect Britain's first Minister of Agriculture, although it was a Board then and he was its Secretary. He was a man of many talents: surveyor, statistician, Fellow of the Royal Society, political commentator, and a keen and observant traveller, who toured France during the Revolution. In his diary he says:

I visited the Maison Carrée, yesterday evening, this morning, and three times during the course of the day. It is . . . the most agreeable

building I have ever seen. Without having an imposing grandeur, or displaying any extraordinary magnificence that might create surprise, it rivets the attention. In its proportions there is a magic harmony that charms the eye. It is impossible to single out any special part for excellence of beauty. It is altogether perfect in symmetry and grace.

During its long history it seems that many people were blind to the qualities that Young saw in it. In the early Middle Ages it served as the local council offices, then as a private house and business premises. The Duchess of Uzès tried to buy it for use as a family mausoleum, but was howled down. Its use as a brothel, however, met with no great objection, and it was later sold to a nobleman who used it to stable his horses. The inner sanctum of the temple houses a small collection of antiquities contemporary with the building. They include a bronze head of Apollo, a huge statue of Apollo, a bust of Jupiter and a marble head of Venus. It is perhaps a coincidence that the design of the Maison Carrée recalls that of the Temple of Apollo in Rome. It was meant for the worship of Augustus, although it was apparently consecrated to his grandsons.

There are more Roman remains in the area of the attractive garden, called the Jardin de la Fontaine. The garden itself was laid out in the 18th century at the foot of a small hill known as Mont Cavalier and around a natural spring. This charming spot was the site in pre-Roman times of a Celtic settlement whose inhabitants worshipped the gods and nymphs of the fountain. When the Romans arrived, they too fell under the spell of the place, which they called Nemausus, and they built their town around it. The spring which gave rise to the original city still gushes out an inexhaustible body of water, which is diverted through channels into the small river Vistre. There are some remains of the spa built by Agrippa during the 1st century AD and the water from the sacred fountain was used to fill the baths. People who today throw coins into the famous Trevi Fountain in Rome, or indeed into any wishing well, are following a custom as old as coins themselves. This spring in the garden at Nîmes has yielded thousands of old coins thrown into it to propitiate the gods.

In addition to Agrippa's spa, there are the ruins of another Roman building, erected about a century later. From an inscription on one of the stones which mentions her name, it is called the Temple of Diana, but it is not really known what was the purpose of this building.

The whole ensemble of the garden, the fountain and the ruins make it an enchanting place, and the modern visitor can still sense something of the magic which made it a place of worship so long ago.

At the top of the hill there is another Roman ruin, called the Tour Magne, which some say was one of a number of watch towers which formed part of the fortifications of the Roman town. Others say it was a single monument to Augustus, similar to the one that exists at La Turbie, on the heights behind Monte Carlo. In either case it is perhaps best appreciated from a distance, as it is unlovely and has little intrinsic interest.

From Nîmes it is a short drive via the N86 and Remoulins to the **Pont du Gard**, and no one visiting any part of the southern Rhône Valley should omit this excursion. In some ways the Pont du Gard is the most splendid of all the Roman remains left to us. It is a simple, concise, and perfect assertion of the Roman ability to get things done, to overcome obstacles, and to combine strength, durability, majesty and elegance in a single structure, and on a massive scale. For those who have not seen it before the Pont du Gard is a surprise, far bigger than most people expect. In spring when the waters of the Gard are often calm, it is reflected almost entirely in the mirror-like surface of the river, a wonderful sight. It stands today virtually as it was 2,000 years ago. It is all that remains of the aqueduct which carried water from the hills near Uzès to Nîmes, but it is not a ruin. It consists of three tiers of arches, super-imposed one on another. The bottom level is 142m long, 6m wide and 22m high, and has six arches. The middle level is 242m long, 4m wide and 20m high, and has eleven arches. The top level is 275m long, 3m wide and 7m high, and has 35 arches. The aqueduct was built about 19BC of huge blocks of stone without cement. Six-ton stones were raised more than 40m, using a system of hoists and pulleys, and manual labour.

The construction of aqueducts to bring limitless supplies of water to their cities was a key characteristic of Roman civilisation, and the Roman builders paid great attention to every detail. The water was collected where-ever possible on the northern slopes of hills, in order to keep its temperature as low as possible in the conduits. The main channel was covered, either vaulted or with flat stone slabs. There were regular openings to ensure that the water was in contact with fresh air, and to enable sections to be cleaned and repaired. Irregularities in the lay of the land were evened out by bridges, trenches, tunnels or syphons.

The aqueduct of which the Pont du Gard formed a part was 50km long, with an average fall of 34cm per kilo-metre, rather more above the Pont du Gard in order to reduce the necessary height of the structure. Over the cen-turies a combination of repeated partial destruction during each of the many attacks on Nîmes, plus the accumulation of limestone deposits in the pipes, gradually made the aqueduct unusable. Once it fell out of use, local inhabitants took stones from it to build houses and churches, and in one case an entire village, and nothing remains of it today apart from

the Pont du Gard itself. In 1743 a road bridge was built against it on the downstream side. It is possible to walk across the top level, either in safety inside the old channel, from which you can see nothing, or on slabs which covered it, which is not recommended for anyone who does not have a good head for heights.

The department of Vaucluse, in which Avignon is situated, gets its name from the Latin *vallis clausa* – 'the closed valley' – which the Romans gave to the mysterious spot now called the **Fontaine de Vaucluse**. Here, at the foot of a 70m horseshoe-shaped cliff, an underground river emerges from a cave into a pool of pale green water surrounded by rocks. The scene is usually calm but at the time of the spring floods the water surges up and bursts over the rocks in cascades. Despite 100 years of searching, the source of this river, the Sorgue, has never been found, though it has been followed by a radio-controlled submarine video-camera to more than 315m below the surface. In the summer months when the water is calm the Fontaine de Vaucluse remains a beauty spot, but unexceptional. Most people will find it disappointing, particularly as it is heavily commer-cialised, and a good example of the less attractive side of tourism.

After Avignon, the last important town on the Rhône before it reaches its delta and the sea is Arles, only 37km distant by the direct route (the N570, then the D79A, then continuing on the N570). But some tourists may like to visit Tarascon en route – for this, stay on the N570 which takes you into Tarascon and out again. This little town, made famous in Alphonse Daudet's *Tartarin de Tarascon* stories, has one of the finest medieval castles in all France. Originally a 13th-century castle, it was entirely rebuilt between 1400 and 1435. It stands on the rocky bank immediately beside the Rhône, and despite its great age is in very good condition. After serving as a prison from the 17th century to 1926, it was completely restored to its condition of 500 years ago. The impressive interior has some good period furniture and Flanders tapestries. The views of the river and far across the surrounding countryside from the terrace above the Rhône are superb.

On the other side of the river, across the unlucky suspension bridge – it was blown down by the mistral in 1845, and blown up in 1944 – now rebuilt, is Beaucaire, another fascinating old town. Though little remains of its château, destroyed on the orders of Richelieu in the early 17th century, Beaucaire still has many fine old stone houses with carved doorways. For hundreds of years Beaucaire was famous as the site of one of the largest commercial fairs in Europe. This fair continued from the Middle Ages until the early part of the 19th century, when industrialisation and the development of railway transport quickly brought it to an end.

Another choice is to travel from Avignon to Arles via the D571 through Châteaurenard, then through St Rémy-de-Provence and Les Baux-de-Provence. **St Rémy** is a charming and typical old Provençal town situated at the foot of Les Alpilles, which have been described as bigger than hills and more beautiful than mountains. Les Alpilles (the little Alps) are known for the range of colours – greys, blues, rose and purple – which their serrated limestone crags reflect in the changing light, particularly at dawn and sunset. St Rémy's great tourist attractions are the Roman remains called Les Antiques, 1km south of the town.

These remains were part of the Roman town of Glanum, destroyed by the Visigoths in the 4th century AD. For some reason they left two monuments untouched. The first, called La Mausolée, was for a long time thought to be the tomb of one of the town's rich merchants and his wife, but it is now believed to be a cenotaph, that is, a memorial not a tomb, to the grandsons of Augustus, Caius and Lucius. The edifice itself dates from about 30BC, but the commemorative inscription referring to Caius and Lucius was probably added at a later date. The monument is in a fine state of preservation. After 2,000 years nothing is missing but the small stone pine-cone ornament from the top.

The triumphal arch is considered to be the most ancient of those in Gaul, and is distinguished by its perfect proportions, and by the quality of its carved ornament. It is believed that it was erected to commemorate Caesar's victories in Gaul.

Opposite Les Antiques are the buildings of the monastery of St Paul-de-Mausole, which was a Franciscan community where the sick were looked after. It was here that Vincent Van Gogh voluntarily had himself confined after a series of mental breakdowns. He stayed there from May 1889 to May 1890. Despite his mental condition he continued to work, painting his room and the immediate surroundings of the monastery. The 12th-century church and its cloister can be visited.

Two hundred metres beyond these monuments is the entrance to the

archaeological site of **Glanum**. Like Nîmes this was originally a Celtic settlement around a sacred spring. It became important during the 4th century BC as a result of contacts with merchants in the Greek colony of Massalia (Marseilles), and the influence of this Greek connection can be seen in the style of some of the private houses, and in the Greek methods of construction used. Later, during the Roman conquest of Gaul, the town became completely Romanised, and the site includes a spa and swimming pool, a forum, temples, Roman as well as Greek houses, fountains and other elements typical of a Roman town.

Close to Les Antiques, a little further down the D5 is situated one of the most extraordinary villages in the whole of France. On top of an isolated spur of rock, thrust out from Les Alpilles, and with steep ravines on either side, **Les Baux-de-Provence** is dramatic, beautiful, a shade sinister and melancholy, all at once. Not many years ago it was a straggle of crumbled and deserted ruins, its walls and towers hard to distinguish from the tormented rock shapes. But the combination of its picturesque site and its history attracted tourists, and now many of its buildings have been restored. New roofs add a touch of colour, and there are even hotels and restaurants. But much of it is still tangled ruins, crowned by the wreck of a castle that seems to grow from the rock itself.

The ramparts of the ruined castle of Les Baux-de-Provence

The best approach to Les Baux is via the D31 and the D27 from St Rémy. Cars must be left outside the village and there is a fair amount of walking, so this is not an excursion that can be hurried. There are hotels in and around the village and it is a place to be experienced at night as well as by day if possible, to be walked around after the last day visitors have left, preferably when a bright moon casts weird shadows and the mistral howls through the broken ramparts like banshees calling for vengeance.

The lords of Les Baux were famous in the Middle Ages, not only for their pride — they claimed descent from Balthazar, one of the Three Wise Men, and took the 16-pointed star of the Nativity as part of their coat of arms — but also for their military strength and riches. At one time more than 80 towns owed them allegiance. They called themselves princes of Baux and adopted many other titles including princes of Orange. It was this last which endured. William, Prince of Orange, became William III of England in 1689.

In the 13th century the court of the princes of Baux was the centre of a brilliant and civilised society. Courts of love, where troubadours gathered to compete in a kind of medieval eisteddfodd with songs in praise of gallantry and courtly love, were held regularly in the seigneurial château. But when Alix, the last princess of Baux died in 1426, Les Baux became a barony and its power and importance rapidly declined. In the 16th century, a de Montmorency, Constable of Provence, became the owner and undertook important restorations of the town. Renaissance houses were built and Les Baux entered on a new

period of prosperity. At the time of the religious wars Les Baux became a Protestant stronghold under the control of the de Manville family. But the king and Richelieu took the Catholic side and Richelieu ordered the destruction of the castle and the ramparts of the town in 1632, and to emphasise the punishment he fined the inhabitants £100,000, which was used to pay the mason who carried out the demolition.

During the Middle Ages the population of Les Baux was about 4,000, but a hundred years ago it was fewer than 30. In the past 20 years, however, tourism has brought a revival and there are now about 400 inhabitants.

Les Baux is packed with interest for anyone with an antiquarian turn of mind. Many of the buildings — the castle, the 12th-century church and some of the Renaissance houses — are classified as historical monuments,

Stone carving is one of the many things to see at Les Baux-de-Provence

and there is a lot more for the curious to discover and find out for themselves. There are even some remains of ancient Roman fortifications, and Roman and Gallo-Roman cemeteries.

Arles is one of the oldest towns in France. In the 6th century BC it was a Celtic settlement which traded with the Phoenicians. When the Greeks founded a colony at Massalia (now Marseilles) at about this time, it was not long before Arles came under their influence and became in effect a Greek city. It was a place where goods being sent up the Rhône were transferred to river boats from sea-going craft and vice versa. Later in Roman times, during the struggle for power between Caesar and Pompey, Marseilles took the side of Pompey, while Arles backed Caesar by supplying boats to help besiege Marseilles. In 49BC Caesar was victorious, and as a reward to Arles settled the veterans of his Sixth Legion there. From that time Arles became a prosperous Roman town. The usual amenities and monuments common to Roman towns were introduced, including a triumphal arch, an arena, a theatre, a forum, a spa, temples, fountains, and an aqueduct bringing fresh water from Les Alpilles. All the streets were paved and the most important were colonnaded. There was a sophisticated drainage system, the main sewer was 3½m in diameter, and even the public lavatories were in white marble and had running water.

After the fall of the Roman Empire, Arles faded into obscurity for several hundred years. Then, when the Emperor Charlemagne died in 814AD, his empire was divided between his descendants and Arles became capital of the part known as Provence-Burgundy,

and once again an important town. In medieval times a new city was built on top of the Roman ruins. Arles continued to prosper so long as the Rhône remained an important transport route, but in the 19th century the development of railways cut traffic on the river to a fraction of what it had been. Arles was ruined.

Writing in 1910, Charles Lentheric, the specialist on the history of the Rhône, said:

> The maritime activity of former days no longer exists. Navigation on the Rhône has been paralysed by the railways. The choked up lagoons have become stagnant marshes.... The whole appearance of the country round Arles has been completely changed, and everything has become vulgar in this town that was formerly patrician.... The splendour of the imperial city no longer reveals itself to us except in its ruins. Like a great number of the ancient towns of the south of France, the 'Rome' of the Gauls is no longer anything but an overgrown village, increasingly vulgar and plebeian in appearance.... Its port is practically deserted, its roads almost empty, its surroundings silent and sad. Solitude and fever surround it. It bestirs itself without dignity and grows old without nobility, becomes extinguished without grandeur. Arles with its bustling population of 25,000 souls is certainly not a dead city but she is a queen dethroned.

This situation continued until after the Second World War, but since then things have steadily improved. Thanks to new light industries and the increase

163

0   50 100 m

Trinquetaille

ARLES

Gare

PL LAMARTINE

RUE DE LA VERRERIE

RUE C. GUYNEMER

RUE DES CAPUCINS

RUE DE LA CAVALERIE

PL VOLTAIRE

RUE PORTAGNEL

BLD EMILE COMBES

RUE DE CAMARGUE

QUAI ST PIERRE

Grand-Rhône

To Montpellier: Nîmes

RUE A BENOÎT

RUE A. TARDIEU

RUE DES GRAND PRIEURE

RUE RASPAIL

PONT DE TRINQUETAILLE

[Quai Marx Dormoy]

RUE DU SAUVAGE

RUE DE L'HÔTEL DE VILLE

RUE DES ARENES

ROND POINT

Arènes

LA LIBERTE

RUE G

PL DU FORUM

RUE DE LA CALADE

DES ARÈNES

Musée Lapidaire Chnetlen

RUE TOUR DE FABRE

Quai de la Roquette

RUE DE LA ROQUETTE

Musée Arlaten

Musée Lapideire Palen

St Trophime

RUE DE CLOITRE

Théâtre Antique

Jardin d'Été

RUE CROIX

RUE RIVES

PL DU BOURG

RUE GALBETTA

RUE DE LA REPUBLIQUE

PL DE LA REPUBLIQUE

BD DES LICES

AV V HUGO

Roman Ramparts

Théâtre

CLEMENCEAU

BD GEORGES

RUE PARMENTIER

PTT

Jardin D'Hiver

AV DES ALYSCAMPS

To Marseille Montpellier Nîmes

To Les Alyscamps

in tourism Arles is prosperous again. The visitor today finds Arles a sunny, inviting, southern city, full of interest and animated by the street cafés of the boulevard des Lices. The most important sights are the amphitheatre or arena, the ancient theatre, St Trophime's church and Les Alyscamps, an old burial ground.

Motorists should follow the N570 into Arles and turn right on to the boulevard des Lices, where there are several parking areas on the southern side; the one near the Post Office is the most convenient. The antique theatre can be reached on foot through the Jardin d'Eté. During the Middle Ages the theatre was completely built over with shops, houses and gardens.

It was not rediscovered until the 17th century and it was the best part of another 200 years before it was excavated. It was found to be in very poor condition, and nothing remained of the stage wall but two tall marble pillars. The stage itself, the orchestra platform, the ditch from which the curtain was raised and part of the original tiers of seats were all that remained of the rest of the theatre.

Restoration has been carried out, particularly of the seating area, and though it is far from complete, no doubt any Roman transported down the centuries would recognise it at once for what it was.

In 1651 workmen digging in the area of the curtain trench unearthed the famous Venus of Arles. It was given as a present to Louis XIV and the original is now in the Louvre, but a moulding of it is in the Pagan section of the Musée Lapidaire in Arles. In the same museum there is a huge statue of Augustus, found about 100 years later, which probably occupied the central niche in the stage wall.

The arena, a short walk from the theatre, was in a far better state of preservation, although, like the one at Nîmes it became a town within a town during the Middle Ages, with people living under the arches and in the galleries, and there were even houses in the central arena and on the old tiers of seats. For a time it served as a fortress and had four watch towers added, of which three are still standing. This amphitheatre, which held more than 20,000 spectators, has two storeys, each with 60 arches. There was originally a third storey, as at Nîmes, but this has completely disappeared. The best way to get a good idea of the size and strength of the whole building is to go up to the platform of the tower above the entrance, which gives you a good view, not only over the arena itself, but also of the town and the surrounding countryside from the Rhône to Les Alpilles.

The arena is in regular use today for public spectacles, particularly bullfighting, which is very popular in the Arles region. Three different styles of bullfights take place there, the *corrida*, the Spanish style in which the bull is killed; the Portuguese, in which the bull is not killed; and the Camarguais, in which the bulls are not killed and appear in numerous fights, and in some cases become better known than the men who fight them.

As a contrast to the classical past of Arles, the church of St Trophime should be visited. Its west door is one of the finest examples of Romanesque sculpture in France. The carving includes the Last Judgement, in the tympanum, above the door, the Twelve Apostles, numerous saints, an angel refusing sinners entry to the gates of Paradise, and another receiving the chosen, all carved in detail with a flowing rhythm and virtuosity. The cloisters of St Trophime are considered to be the finest in Provence. The north and east galleries are Romanesque and date from the end of the 12th century, those on the south and west are Gothic, about 100 years later.

The pillars at the east and west corners of the north gallery are especially well carved. It is thought that some of the stones used in the construction of these cloisters were taken from the dump formed by Cyrillus in the 5th century. The interior of the church is distinguished by the fine proportions of the nave, narrow but more than 20m high and well lit from above.

Keen students of religious art may like to compare St Trophime with St Gilles, 16km west of Arles on the N572, where the façade has three superb arches linked by a frieze which from left to right gives the story of Holy Week, from the entry of Jesus into Jerusalem to the Crucifixion. Below the frieze and between the pillars there are carvings of the apostles and saints, and other scenes including the murder of Abel by Cain.

Arles must be one of the few places which has a cemetery which is a tourist attraction, at least to those visitors with an interest in history. Les

The cloisters of St Tromphime in Arles are considered to be some of the finest in Provence

Alyscamps is situated in a rather seedy commercial quarter in the southern part of the city. It was already a famous cemetery in Roman times and not only continued to be a burial place in early Christian era, but in the Middle Ages became the most fashionable cemetery in Europe. More and more of the faithful sought to be buried there until there were thousands of tombs, and in places they were stacked one on top of another. It was so popular that at one time there were 19 churches and chapels in Les Alyscamps. It is said that it was the custom to float coffins down the

Beneath the Roman arena, Arles

Rhône, with a sum of money inside them as a burial fee. At Arles they were collected at the Trinquetaille port and taken to Les Alyscamps.

Some of the early stone tombs were such masterpieces of carving that in the 16th century local social climbers adopted the habit of making gifts of these antique sarcophagi to the princes of various districts and other notables they wished to influence, an unusual form of bribe easily acquired by a more formal gift to a cemetery official. Within the next 100 years so many of the best tombs were taken that the authorities decided to protect those that remained by removing them to the comparative safety of different churches. Some of the best, dating from the 2nd and 3rd centuries AD, can be seen in the Pagan section of the Musée Lapidaire, and there are also some of slightly later date in the Christian section of this museum.

Despite its unattractive surroundings Les Alyscamps has an atmosphere of its own, enclosed in a leafy glade of poplars, cypresses and acacias, where nightingales sing and in late spring the white acacia petals drift down over the last of the ancient tombs. The Romanesque church of St Honorat, which presides over this strange place, has been a ruin for 1,000 years. Its restoration was started in 1175 but was never finished. In Les Alyscamps the past is ever present, a persistent sad echo down the years.

Apart from the delightful Alpilles to the north-east, Arles is surrounded by some of the dullest countryside in all France. To the south-east is the 200km^2 of the plain of La Crau, still largely a desert of huge pebbles, though in the northern part some areas have been made suitable for cultivation. On the other side of the Rhône, west and south to the sea, is the region known as the Camargue. Here the Rhône, which began its long journey with such impetuous force, loses itself in a morass of aimless wandering, pouring half its waters into dozens of small streams, bogs, marshes, and extensive shallow lagoons.

For long famous for its wild if monotonous labyrinth of land and water, and for the rich wildlife found there, the Camargue is not what it used to be. The character of its northern part has been much changed since the Second World War by successful drainage of extensive marshy areas and the cleansing of salt from the soil. Following this, many thousands of hectares were turned over to rice

production, but today this is only a tenth of what it was in the sixties, and maize, vines and vegetables are grown in its place. In the southern Camargue salt has been produced since antiquity, by allowing sea water to evaporate in shallow lagoons. In recent years this industry has also expanded and cut into wild areas of the Camargue. There are now well over 20,000ha devoted to salt, producing over a million tons a year.

As the size of the wild and untouched Camargue has been reduced, so has its character been altered. It was traditionally a place where the black bulls were bred for the arenas of Arles and the Languedoc. Some of these ranches do still exist, but there are now many of what in the American West would be called 'dude' ranches. They offer riding holidays and too many of these ranches are touristic in the poor sense of the word.

But the central southern Camargue is still a maze of intercommunicating water — lagoons, marshes, and channels leading eventually to the sea. Here, the varied wildlife of the Camargue still exists. Ornithologists count up to 400 different kinds of birds, 160 of them migratory. There are also wild boar, beavers, coypu, otters, water tortoises, rabbits and other small species. In the early 1970s the Parc Naturel Régional de la Camargue was set up in an attempt to protect the wildlife against the inroads of tourism, agriculture and industry. It is a losing, though not yet a lost, battle. The park includes the whole of the large Etang de Vaccarès and the area south of it to the sea coast. It is open to accredited ornithologists and students of natural history, but not to members of the general public.

The casual visitor to the Camargue is unlikely to see any of the animals mentioned, unless by the purest chance. But there are still numbers of flamingoes outside the park, and motorists who make a tour of the Camargue, which takes the best part of a day, would be quite likely to see some. Binoculars are useful, because the lagoons are often of considerable size and the birds too far out in them to be clearly seen with the naked eye. But at Pont de Gau, just north of Stes Maries-de-la-Mer, there is a bird sanctuary open to the public. It covers 12ha of marsh, where most birds native to the Camargue can be seen in their natural habitat. There are signposted footpaths, and only a few of the more elusive species are kept in huge aviaries; the rest are at liberty.

The animals which all visitors to the Camargue are likely to see are the famous white horses and black bulls. Each of these animals belongs to a special race of obscure origin, cloaked in legend (see box).

Stes Maries-de-la-Mer, the traditional 'capital' of the Camargue, is a rather characterless town trying hard to become a tourist resort. Its beach is spacious, shadeless, and exposed to every wind that blows, especially the mistral.

Because of its legendary holy origin (see box) Stes Maries has been a place of pilgrimage since the earliest days of Christianity. In 1448 King René of

Black Bulls and White Horses

Though most of the animals of the Camargue are discreet and difficult to see without patience and luck, all visitors are likely to see some black bulls and white horses. Each of these animals belong to a special race of obscure origin, cloaked in legend.

The white horses are said by the local people to be descended from the horses which drew Neptune's chariot, and it is certainly true that they are happy in water. People of more prosaic spirit suggest that they are of part-Arab blood, descended from horses brought back from the Middle East by Crusaders, or from horses brought into France by Saracen invaders in the 8th century. Whatever the legend, the fact is that they are rather small horses of great stamina, and they are born with a brown coat which does not turn completely white until they are about four years old.

It is not known how the black bulls of the Camargue came to France. They are much smaller than Spanish bulls, and have lyre-shaped horns carried high on the head, unlike the widely spaced and lower-set horns of the Spanish race. The black bull of the Camargue is in fact the same bull as can be seen in effigy at Knossos in Crete. It is the bull of Mithras, and may have been brought into France by the first Roman or Greek invaders, many of whom were followers of the Mithraic religion, the worship of the god of the harvest. It may well have been a bull of this race, that the Romans used to drag St Sernin to his death through the streets of Toulouse, after he refused to take part in its sacrifice.

Provence ordered that a search should be made for the remains of the saints, whose bodies were said to have been buried in the choir of the church during the Saracen invasions of the 9th century. The relics were 'found' and from that time the pilgrimages became more important. It was not until the 19th century that the community took the name Stes Maries-de-la-Mer, and though gypsies have visited the Camargue since about the 15th century, it was not until the 19th century that the annual gathering of gypsies from all over Europe began.

Nowadays about 10,000 gypsies come for the pilgrimage, when on 24 May the relics are brought from the chapel and watched over, and then on the 25th they are paraded through the streets to the shore, together with the statue of Sarah, the Egyptian servant, the gypsies' own saint. The procession is followed by the gypsies and the faithful, and in addition to the officials of the church with the holy relics there are Arlesiennes in their lovely costume, and an escort of *gardians* the 'cowboys' of the Camargue. This first pilgrimage is associated with the festival of Mary Jacoby, and there is a second, more local affair, for the festival of Mary Salome, on the Saturday and Sunday nearest 22 October.

In the 9th century a church was built to replace the oratory said to

Drifting Boats

Though it is rather lacking in charm, Stes Maries-de-la-Mer is not devoid of interest. It gets its name, which it took rather belatedly about 100 years ago, from an ancient legend. According to this story, in about 40BC the Jews expelled from Jerusalem Mary Salome, the mother of the apostles James and John, and Mary Jacoby, the sister of the Virgin, and their servant, Sarah, a dark-skinned Egyptian. They were cast adrift in a boat without oars or sails, and with no food. With God's protection and guidance they survived and eventually drifted ashore at what is now Stes Maries-de-la-Mer, where they set up the first oratory to the Virgin.

If this story is compared with the legend of St James of Compostella, it seems that the family had a penchant for drifting boats. In that story James, the brother of John, was shipwrecked on the coast of Galicia in northern Spain. He stayed there seven years spreading Christianity and then returned to the Holy Land, where he died in 44AD. His disciples are said to have placed his body in a boat which they cast adrift and which was divinely steered to the place in Galicia where he had first been shipwrecked. There he was buried, and his tomb was venerated for 300 years, and then forgotten. Six hundred years later, says the legend, holy men set out to find it again, which they did, guided by a moving star – hence the name of the place, *campus stellae*, the field of the star. St James of Compostella was, after the Holy Land itself, the most important Christian place of pilgrimage throughout the Middle Ages, and is still a place of pilgrimage today.

Modern scholars gave little credence to either of these legends.

have been raised in honour of the Virgin Mary by the saints, and which is known to have been there in the 6th century. But the remarkable church one sees today was built towards the end of the 12th century and was extended in the 15th. It is in an attractive golden stone, and formed part of the fortifications of the town. It looks as much like a fortress as a church, with a high keep and battlements. The nave contains a well, so that in times of siege those who took refuge in the church would have water.

Near the church, installed in the former Town Hall, there is a small museum, the Musée Baroncelli, devoted to the history and life of the Camargue. The collection was put together by the Marquis Folco de Baroncelli, a breeder of bulls and rancher of the Camargue, who did much to revive its old traditions and customs, and to perpetuate its special character

Throughout the summer boat trips are available up the Petit Rhône from Stes Maries-de-la-Mer, and this is perhaps the best way of appreciating the watery vastness and special character of the Camargue. The black bulls and white horses graze in pastures beside the banks. Herons, moorhens and ducks of all kinds, and sometimes flamingoes, haunt the reed beds, and the horizons vanish in a mirage of heat haze.

Away on the other side of the Camargue, the Grand Rhône flows past an utterly different world. The horizon here is blocked by oil refineries, enormous chemical factories, steel mills and gigantic port installations. The throb of engines and the clang of metal reverberate across the water. When night falls, the floodlights of incessant labour are reflected on the surface, and the red flames of oil burn away the night sky. Where Phoenician and Roman galleys sailed 2,000 years ago, great ships still come and go, night and day, and the wide Rhône rolls on. Gone by, the ice and the mountains. Gone by, the ancient cities, the Roman temples, the ruined castles. Gone by, the Renaissance churches, the quiet villages and their fruitful fields. Gone by, the stones of history. The great river slides on, silent and sedate now, to the waiting sea.

Hotels & Restaurants

Prices: A = Very Expensive, B = Expensive, C = Moderately Expensive, D = Average, E = Cheap.

ARLES (13200 Bouches-du-Rhône): **Jules César**, 7 bld des Lices (90 93 43 20). For those who like and can afford the best. Converted 17th-century Carmelite monastery. Heated swimming pool, and one of the best restaurants in Provence. Relais et Châteaux. Rooms and meals A.
Mireille, 2 pl St Pierre (90 93 70 74). Just across the river in the Trinquetaille quarter, but one of the very few in Arles with a restaurant. Modern. Patio and swimming pool. Rooms and meals C–E.
Le Flamant Rose, Albaron, 13123 (90 97 10 18). Simple and charming Logis de France, about 12km south-west of Arles in the northern Camargue. Very well run, and good country cooking by madame la patronne. Shady terrace. (Only a few rooms with bath). Rooms and meals D–E.
La Paillote, 28 rue du Docteur Fanton (90 96 33 15). Traditional cuisine well executed. In the town centre. Meals C–D.
La Côte d'Adam, 12 rue de la Liberte (90 49 62 29). Sound, not uninspired, and affordable. Town centre. Meals D–E.

AVIGNON (84000 Vaucluse): **L'Europe**, 12 pl Crillon (90 82 66 92). Quiet and luxurious hotel in what was a nobleman's mansion. Prestigious restaurant, La Vieille Fontaine. Avignon's best. Rooms A–C. Meals B. (Restaurant closed one week in August.)
D'Angleterre, 29 bld Raspail (90 86 34 31). Well-established, traditional. A Logis de France member but without restaurant. Rooms D–E.
Fimotel, 8–14 bld St Dominique (90 82 08 08). Large modern hotel just outside the walls. Rooms D. Meals D–E.
Le Vernet, 58 rue Joseph Vernet (90 86 64 53). The place to dine on a summer evening beneath old trees in a large garden. *Haute cuisine* at a reasonable price. Meals C–D.
Le Petit Bedon, 70 rue Joseph Vernet (90 82 33 98). Two menus only and no *carte*, but good value. (Closed last 2 weeks of June.) Meals C–D.
L'Entrée des Artistes, 1 pl des Carmes (90 82 46 90). Lively, worth trying to get a table on the terrace. Sound and unpretentious meals. Meals D.

LES BAUX-DE-PROVENCE (13520 Bouches-du-Rhône): **Bautezar**, rue Fréderic Mistral (90 54 32 09). Comfortable and charming small hotel in the village itself. Rooms D. Meals D+.
La Benvengudo, route d'Arles (90 54 32 54). Peaceful, romantic situation in its own park. Very comfortable, with excellent restaurant. Tennis and swimming pool. Rooms C–D+. Meals C.
Oustau de Baumanière (90 54 33 07). One of the great restaurants of France. Everything in the grand manner, from the period furniture to the stylish and

impeccable cooking. Luxurious small Relais et Châteaux hotel attached. Home from home for spendthrift millionaires. Meals A.

CHATEAUNEUF-DU-PAPE (84230 Vaucluse): **La Garbure**, 3 rue Joseph Ducos (90 83 75 08). Good restaurant in an old vaulted wine cellar. First-class and original dishes. Meals C–D.

NÎMES (30000 Gard): **Mercure**, 113 chemin de L'Hostellerie (66 84 14 55). Near the western exit of the autoroute. Large, well-equipped modern hotel (swimming pool, tennis, garden). Rooms and meals D.
Campanile, chemin de la Carreras, Cassargues, 30132 (66 84 27 05). Modern chain hotel well situated at Cassargue a few kilometres south of Nîmes on the D42, the Nîmes–St Gilles road. Rooms and meals D.
L'Enclos de la Fontaine, quai de la Fontaine (66 21 90 30). *Haute cuisine* at fair prices. Near the sights. Meals B–C.
San Francisco, 33 rue Roussy (66 21 00 80). French version of a steak house. Business orientated and closed for three weeks in August. Good value when open. Meals C–D.
San Francisco Wine Bar, 11 square de la Couronne (66 76 19 59). French version of a wine bar or pub. Near the above and under same management, but cheaper. Good wines by the glass. Meals D.

ORANGE (84100 Vaucluse): **Arène**, pl des Langes (90 34 10 95). Calm hotel in a shady square in the town centre. Nice terrace. No restaurant. Rooms D.

ST RÉMY-DE-PROVENCE (13210 Bouches-du-Rhône): **Auberge de la Reine Jeanne**, 12 bld Mirabeau (90 92 15 33). Typically Provençal inn, tastefully installed in an 18th-century house. Rooms D. Meals D–E.
Château de Roussan, route de Tarascon (90 92 11 63), 2km north of St Rémy on N99. Beautifully furnished country house in a lovely park. No restaurant. Rooms C–D.
Les Arts, 30 bld Victor Hugo (90 92 08 50). Good restaurant in a genuine Provençal atmosphere. Meals D.

VAISON-LA-ROMAINE (84110 Vaucluse): **Hostellerie le Beffroi**, Haute Ville (90 36 04 71). Good hotel in lovely Renaissance house in the old town. Some rooms with fine views. Rooms C–E. Meals D.
Domaine de Cabasse, Seguret (90 46 91 12), 9km south-west of Vaison via D977 and D88. A farmhouse inn among vineyards. Well equipped and furnished. Rooms with obligatory half-board C–D. Meals C.

VILLENEUVE-LES-AVIGNON (30400 Gard): **Residence les Cèdres**, 39 bld Pasteur (90 25 43 92). Pleasant Logis de France. Rooms D–E. Meals D.
L'Atelier, 5 rue de la Foire (90 25 01 84). Charming and cosy hotel in the centre of Villeneuve. No restaurant.

Museums, Châteaux, Sites etc: opening times

Note: am/pm means closed for lunch (normally for two hours).

ARLES: Opening times are standardised for the arena, the ancient theatre, the St Trophime cloister, the Musée Lapidaire, Les Alyscamps, etc.) All day from the beginning of May to the end of Sept. Individual tickets or cheap rate for all monuments.

AVIGNON: Palace of the Popes, all day July–Sept inclusive. Am/pm Easter to the end of June. Rest of the year accompanied visits only am/pm. Some parts of the Palace are closed to visitors.
Petit Palais, am/pm. Closed Tues and public holidays.
Pont St Bénézet and St Nicholas chapel, am/pm. Closed Tues (except June, July and Aug) and Jan and Feb.
Musée Calvet, am/pm. Closed Tues, and some public holidays.

CAMARGUE: Tourists wishing to visit the Parc Naturel de la Camargue, who should be bona fide naturalists, should enquire at the Centre d'Information de la Capelière, on the D36B to the east of the Etang de Vaccarès, 13200 Arles. Open am/pm Mon–Fri.

NÎMES: Roman monuments (Arena, Maison Carrée, Tour Magne), all day from mid-June to mid-Sept. Am/pm rest of the year. Visits to the arena suspended for duration of spectacles, bullfights etc.

ORANGE: Roman theatre, open all day at weekdays April to Sept am/pm on Sun. Am/pm every day for the rest of the year. Ticket also gives admission to the town museum.

ST RÉMY-DE-PROVENCE: Roman ruins of Glanum, am/pm all year except public holidays.

VAISON-LA-ROMAINE: Roman ruins, am/pm all year round. One ticket covers all monuments.

Leisure

Birdwatching in the Camargue; bullfights at Arles in the Roman arena; boat trips on the Petit Rhône in the Camargue; pony trekking; gliding. Details of these activities, and dates, are obtainable from the local tourist offices.

Tourist Information Offices

AVIGNON — 41 cours Jean Jaures (90 82 65 11).

ARLES — 35 pl de la République (90 93 49 11).

NÎMES — 6 rue Auguste (66 67 29 11).

Index

Abbans, Marquis Jouffroy de 49
Adhémar family 127, 129–32
Agrippa 9, 45, 157
Aiguebelette, Lac d' 37–8
Aix-les-Bains 24, 38–9
Albertville 30–1
Allan 127
Alpine Garden 111
Alps 109–14
Amédée VI, Count of Savoy
    (Green Count) 23, 30
Amédée VII, Count of Savoy
    (Red Count) 23, 30
Amédée VIII, Duke of Savoy
    (later Pope Felix V) 23, 30
Ampère, André Marie 62
Annecy 24–5
Annecy, Lac d' 25–6
Annecy-le-Vieux 25
Les Antiques 159, 161
aqueducts 46, 157–8
Ardèche 74–94
    caves 90–3
    Gorges de l' 90
    river 3
Arkwright, Captain 32
Arles 163–8
Aubenas 84
Augustus, Emperor 9, 45
Avignon 146–54

Balazuc 87
Baronnies region 135
Bartholdi, Auguste 60
Les Baux-de-Provence 160–3
Bayard 102, 104
Beaucaire 159
Béconne 128
La Bégude-de-Mazenc 127
Benedict XIII, Pope 148–9
Bénézet, St 150–1
Berlioz, Hector 106–7
Bernard de Menthon, St 27–8
Black Death 46, 147

boats, river 13, 15–17
Bourdeaux 128
Le Bourg d'Oisans 110
Bourg-de-Péage 124
Bourgelat, Claude 48
Bourget, Lac du 24, 39
Bourne, Gorges de la 115
bridges 15–16, 79, 151, 152–3
Buis-les-Baronnies 136
bulls, black 168, 169
Burgondes 9, 46
Burney, Charles 38–9

Caligula, Emperor 46
Camargue, the 3, 168–71
Carthusians 107, 108–9
Catherine de Medici, Queen 11
caves 90–3, 115
Celts 8–9, 161
Chambéry 35–6
Chambonas 93
La Chambotte 40
Chamonix 31
Charles IX, King of France 11
Charles Albert, King of Savoy and Sardinia
    30–1
Les Charmettes 35, 37
chartreuse liqueur 108–9
Châteauneuf-de-Mazenc 127
Châteauneuf-du-Pape 147
Chorance caves 115
Cinq-Mars, Marquis de 61
Claudius, Emperor 46, 57
Clement V, Pope 147
Clement VI, Pope 147, 148
Clovis, King of the Franks 9, 46, 51
Combe de Laval 116
Condrieu 75
Conflans 31
La Côte-St André 106–7
Crest 124–5
Cruas 82–3
Crussol, Château de 80

176

Daudet, Alphonse 88, 158
Dauphiné, the 99–100, 124
Dickens, Charles 57
Die 125–6
Dieulefit 127–8, 129
Les Dombes 64
Donzère-Mondragon hydroelectric works 17–18, 126, 132
Drac valley 101
Drôme 121–36
Duèze, Cardinal Jacques (later Pope John XXII) 147
Duingt 27
Durance, river 3
Durand family 83

Ecrins, Parc National des 111, 114
Escalin, Antoine 132
Etang de Vaccarès 168
Evelyn, John 17
Evian-les-Bains 29–30

Fier, Gorges du 28
food 19–21
François I, King of France 23, 47
Franks 9, 46

La Garde-Adhémar 132
Glanum 159, 161
La Grand Chartreuse 107–9
Grand Goulets 116
La Grave 110–11
Greeks 8, 163
Gregory XI, Pope 147–8
Grenfell, Gerard Morgan 18
Grenoble 99–103
Grignan 129–32
Gryphis, Sebastien 47
Guiers Mort 108

Hardouin-Mansart, Jules 60
Hautecombe, Abbaye de 39–40
Henri II, King of France 23
Henri III, King of France 11
Henri IV, King of France 11–12, 48, 86
Henri Malartre Vintage Car Museum 63
horses 169
Humbert II, Dauphin 99–100
hydroelectricity 17–18, 100

Isère 98–117
river 3

Jacquard, M. 49
James of Compostella, St 170
Jeanne, Queen of Naples 147, 148

John XXII, Pope 147
Jongkind, Johan Barthold 107
Jussieu, Antoine, Bernard and Joseph de 48

Labeaume 87–8
Lamastre 78
Lentheric, Charles 163
le Roy, Guillaume 47
Lesdiguieres, François de Bonne, Duc de 100, 104
Louis IX, King of France 13
Louis XIII, King of France 12, 61, 125
Louis, Prince of Hungary 148
Lyon 2, 9, 45–63
    Fairs 11, 47, 48
    history 12, 45–51
    museums 57, 60–2
    printing 47
    textiles 47, 49–50, 62
    traboules 56
Lyonnais 44, 63–9

Mandrin, Louis 123
Marcieu, Monteynard de, family 106
Maries, Stes 169–71
Marseilles 8, 163
Martel, Charles 46
Marzal, Aven de 92
Le Mas de la Vignasse 88
Massif Central 77
Megève 33
Menthon-St Bernard 27–8
Merimée, Prosper 133
Mollans-sur-Ouvèze 135
Mont Blanc 31–3
Montélimar 126
Montgolfier brothers 48–9
Montrottier, Château de 28–9
Moors 46
Moulin, Jean 51
La Mure, railway 105, 106

Napoleon 49, 51, 80, 136
Napoleon III 24, 39
Naves 94
Nîmes 154–7
Nyons 134–5

Orange 143–6
Orange, princes of 162
Orgnac, Aven d' 91–2

Païolive, Bois de 93
Parc National de la Vanoise 24, 33–5
Parc National des Ecrins 111, 114

Parc Naturel Régional de Camargue
3, 168–71
Parc Naturel Régional de Vercors 114–15
Pérouges 63–4
La Perte du Rhône 2
Philip, the Good, King of France 46
Phoenicians 8
Pierregourde, Château de 80–2
Pierrelongue 135–6
Plancus 9, 45
Le Poët-Laval 127–8
Point, Fernand 67
Pont d'Arc 88–9
Pont du Gard 157–8
Pont-en-Royans 115
Pont-St Esprit 15, 17
popes 147–9
printing 47
Privas 83–4
Provence 140–71

Religion, Wars of 9, 11–12, 48, 81, 83,
84, 162
Revolution 12, 49
Rhône, river 1–4
bridges 15–16, 79, 151, 152–3
history 12–18
Ripaille, Domaine de la 30
Rochecolombe 87
Romans 8–9, 12, 157–8
Aix 39
aqueducts 46, 157–8
Arles 164–5, 167
Grenoble 99
Lyon 9, 45–6, 57, 60
Nîmes 154–7
Orange 143–6
remains 10, 39, 57, 60, 141–6 154–8,
164–5
roads 110
St Rémy 159, 161
Vaison-la-Romaine 141–3
Valence 121
Vienne 8–9, 10, 45
Romans-sur-Isère 124
Rousseau, Jean-Jacques 37
Ruoms 87

St Christophe-en-Oisans 114
St Hugues church 107–8
Stes Maries-de-la-Mer 169–71
St Nazaire-en-Royans 124
St Paul-Trois-Châteaux 133
St Rémy 159
St Romain-de-Lerps 80
Saône 2

Sardinia 24
Savarin, Brillat 19
Savoy 2, 22–43
history 22–4
schism, great Western 147–9
Seguin, Marc 15–16, 79
Serres, Olivier de 86, 126
Serrières 75
Sévigné, Marie, Marquise de 130
smuggling 123
steamboats 16–17, 49
Stendhal 19, 104
Suze-la-Rousse 133–4

Tain-l'Hermitage 78, 124
Tarascon 158–9
Taulignan 129
Tendret, Lucien 19
textiles 47, 49–50, 62
Thines 94
Thonon-les-Bains 30
Tournon 77–8
Le Touvet, Château 105–6
traboules 56
Tricastin nuclear power station 132
truffles 129

Umberto II, King of Italy 23, 24
Utrecht, Treaty of 23–4

Vaison-la-Romaine 141–3
Val des Nymphes 133
Valence 121–4
Valois dynasty 11–12
Vals-les-Bains 84–5
Van Gogh, Vincent 159
Vanoise National Park 24, 33–5
Les Vans 93
Vassieux-en-Vercors 116–17
Vaucluse, Fontaine de 158
Ventoux, Mont 143
Vercors, Parc Naturel Régional de 114–15
Victor Emmanuel II, King of Italy 24
Vienne 8–9, 64–9
Villard-de-Lans 115
Villeneuve-les-Avignon 154
Vizille, Château 104–5
Vogüé 86–7

walking, mountain 34–5, 114
weather 4–5
Whymper, Edward 32
wine 21, 78, 124, 125
World War II 12, 51, 104, 116

Young, Arthur 156